Alice Hayes, George Gilbert Maclaren

My Leper Friends

An Account of Personal Work Among Lepers and of their Daily Life in India

Alice Hayes, George Gilbert Maclaren

My Leper Friends

An Account of Personal Work Among Lepers and of their Daily Life in India

ISBN/EAN: 9783337473464

Printed in Europe, USA, Canada, Australia, Japan

Cover: Foto ©Thomas Meinert / pixelio.de

More available books at **www.hansebooks.com**

MY LEPER FRIENDS.

AN ACCOUNT OF
PERSONAL WORK AMONG LEPERS, AND OF THEIR DAILY LIFE IN INDIA.

By Mrs. M. H. HAYES.

WITH A CHAPTER ON LEPROSY,

BY SURGEON-MAJOR G. G. MACLAREN, M.D.

ILLUSTRATED.

LONDON:
W. THACKER AND CO., 87, NEWGATE STREET.
CALCUTTA: THACKER, SPINK AND CO.
BOMBAY: THACKER AND CO., LIMITED.

1891.

PREFACE.

THE objects I had in view when writing this book were to interest the public in the white lepers who are homeless in India, and to obtain money for the "Leper Fund" which I raised, and which is now being administered by the Very Reverend Archdeacon Michell, of Calcutta. My publishers, Messrs. Thacker & Co., 87, Newgate Street, E.C., have kindly consented to forward to this gentleman any profit that may accrue from the sale of the book, which, on this account, I trust will be large. I venture to think that, apart from the good intent, all classes of readers will find this small work worthy of perusal, in that it is a series of true pictures of a very sad phase of human misery, namely, the inner life of sufferers whom I have known so well and have cared for so much, that I can in all sincerity call them "My Leper Friends."

I hear, with deep regret, that, since my departure from India, subscriptions to the "Leper Fund" have decreased. As it is the means of brightening the lives of the most wretched of all human beings, I would appeal to the generosity of the public to support it by sending contributions to Archdeacon Michell, Calcutta, who personally superintends the distribution of the fund. I may mention that aid is given without any distinction as to creed.

My best thanks are due to Dr. G. G. MacLaren for his sympathy in my labours, and for his kindness in writing a chapter on leprosy for this book. I, also, am glad of this opportunity of expressing my great indebtedness to "Brother John," who was my fellow-worker among the lepers and in the hospitals of Calcutta.

I shall be happy to answer inquiries on this subject. My address is, care of Messrs. W. Thacker & Co., 87, Newgate Street, London, E.C.

ALICE HAYES.

LONDON, 3rd *September*, 1891.

CONTENTS.

CHAPTER I.
Settling in Calcutta—Our "Sporting News"... ... 1—4

CHAPTER II.
Brother John—Mr. McGuire—Government officials—The leper asylum—An Irish woman—The Jewess—Daisy and Bella—A death scene—Eurasian lepers ... ... 5—23

CHAPTER III.
The account I wrote—Bridget—An official visit to the lepers ... ... 24—33

CHAPTER IV.
Newspaper criticism—"Truth" and Mr. Prinsep—"The Queen" ... ... 34—38

CHAPTER V.
Efforts to comfort—Our subscription fund—Improvements ... ... 39—47

CHAPTER VI.
Miss O'Brien—Amateur actors—A performance in aid of our fund ... ... 48—55

CONTENTS.

	PAGE
CHAPTER VII.	
White lepers—Dr. McLaren—Heat and misery	56—62
CHAPTER VIII.	
Need for a home for European and Eurasian lepers—Our public meeting	63—73
CHAPTER IX.	
Hope—Kate Reilly	74—80
CHAPTER X.	
Archdeacon Michell—Disposal of our fund—The leper cat—The idiot boy	81—88
CHAPTER XI.	
The nuns of Loretto Convent...	89—94
CHAPTER XII.	
Medicine—No warm baths—An ugly looking-glass—Christmas-day in the Leper Asylum—The leper boy—Mr. Bailey	95—111
CHAPTER XIII.	
Lepers in Bombay—A lecture at the Sorosis Club—Our departure from India ...	113—119
CHAPTER XIV.	
Remarks on Leprosy, by Surgeon-major G. G. MacLaren, M.D....	120—127

MY LEPER FRIENDS.

CHAPTER I.

SETTLING IN CALCUTTA—OUR "SPORTING NEWS."

In the early summer of 1888 my husband and I found ourselves enjoying a well-earned holiday in Japan. He, I may explain, writes books about horses, which have rendered his name widely known among English readers; and having a special talent for making these animals conform to his wishes, he conceived the idea of going on a tour, with the object of teaching all he knew about "breaking" to those interested in the subject. In England, horses, as a rule, are so well "made" that the equine instructor finds much difficulty in illustrating his lessons. But abroad the case is very different. In India he had, during the year he was there, hundreds of buck-jumpers, man-eaters, jibbers, and other refractory creatures, the subjugation of which gained him great credit, as well as a goodly sum of money. Even in China, from which we had just come, there were plenty of examples among the sturdy Mongolian ponies to test his skill and patience. When a horse or pony, which previously would not allow anyone to mount him, was reduced to obedience in an hour or two, a side-saddle was usually put on him, and then I mounted him, took up the reins, put him through his paces, and jumped him over some improvised fences. Although our work "caught on" wherever we went, it proved somewhat monotonous, and I longed for a settled home after this continued round of hotel and steamer life. My husband wanted to go to California, and then on to New York, while I suggested India, where I had spent a pleasant time in the indulgence of my then hobby— theatricals. In those days I looked upon my dear old teachers—Mr. Hermann Vezin, Mr. John MacLean, and Miss Glyn Dallas—as the greatest of man and woman-kind, and thought more of a favourable notice in some obscure local print of my acting, than of the praise in the *Field* and *Graphic* accorded to my riding, when my husband gave a performance at Neasden, near London, in aid of the funds for the "Home of Rest for Horses." Knowing what a charm novelty had for my husband, and wishing to get back to India, I suggested the advisability of his going to Calcutta and starting there a sporting paper, which, with his name as editor, would be sure to draw! My counsel proved so acceptable that I had only barely time to pack up my boxes and get them on board the French mail, for which my husband had taken tickets. We arrived at Calcutta, started our paper, and, in a short time, settled down to our work as journalists. This came easy to my husband, as he had been connected with the press for many years, and not very difficult to me, as I was deeply interested in the success of our venture, and had been accustomed, during my travels, to write articles for various papers. My rôle on our *Sporting News* was that of dramatic and musical critic, as well as that of describing events of passing interest, with a certain dash of sporting flavour, from a lady's point of view. The habit of observation which was forced on me probably sobered down my thoughts a good deal;

for I was gradually led to pay more and more attention to the sadder aspects of human life, which were but too common around me. In India, I found death was such an intimate acquaintance that his terrors, in the case of others, were too often regarded with callous indifference; and that the fact of the English residents being but temporary sojourners made them disinclined to support permanent charitable institutions, although they are extremely liberal, at the time, when personally appealed to, in the cause of suffering humanity. With the view of counteracting the apathy displayed by the local public towards its institutions for the good of the poor, and to furnish readable "copy" to our paper, I began a series of articles called "Calcutta Charities." One day while I was writing, my husband came back from a visit to an old broken-down jockey, who used, many years ago, to ride for him, and who was then living in the Calcutta Almshouse. He told me all he had seen in this institution, and I became so interested in it that I resolved to call and see its female inmates.

CHAPTER II.

BROTHER JOHN—MR. McGUIRE—GOVERNMENT OFFICIALS—THE LEPER ASYLUM—AN IRISH WOMAN—THE JEWESS—DAISY AND BELLA—A DEATH SCENE—EURASIAN LEPERS.

I TOOK with me, on the occasion of my visit to the almshouse, a friend, Brother John, of the Society of St. Paul, who was engaged in the work of the Calcutta Seamen's Mission, under the direction of his superior, the Reverend Father Hopkins. I became acquainted with Brother John through Father Hopkins, who called and asked me to sing at one of his weekly concerts for sailors in Bentinck Street, arranging to send Brother John to take me to the place in a cab. Father Hopkins said, "You must not be shocked on finding the brother a rough sailor, who drops his 'h's' and is afraid of women, never having been accustomed to ladies' society. You will find he has a good heart. The sailors all like Brother John." On the evening appointed, the brother arrived with the cab for me. He was shown into our drawing-room, and was evidently keeping those refractory "h's" of his well under control, for I could not get him to talk at all, and thought him rather stupid, as he sat nervously clutching his hat. Afterwards, when he knew me better, he told me that he suffered agonies on that evening, and begged Father Hopkins not to depute him to fetch me, but to send, instead, Brother Paul, who knew how to behave to ladies. Poor Brother John little knew me, if he thought that the mere fact of his being insufficiently educated would render me heedless of the many good traits in his fine character! I liked him as soon as he had overcome his nervousness enough to permit of his saying, "I hope you'll excuse me if I'm not accustomed to ladies' society. I'm only a rough sailor, and I don't know how to speak or what to say to ladies. I get along all right with the sailors. I've never had any education, and I feel the want of it now badly." This honest speech of his made me his friend at once, and I often went to the sailors' concerts after that night. He was one of nature's gentlemen, who seemed always able to say and do the right thing instinctively, and whose quiet, simple manner would command the respect of his fellows. I used to like going with Brother John every week to visit the sick sailors in the Calcutta hospitals. On such occasions he would provide a good supply of plug tobacco (beloved of Jack) and newspapers. It was while going our weekly round one day that I mentioned my intended visit to the almshouse, and arranged with him to accompany me.

When we arrived at the place, we were shown into the office of a soldierly-looking man of about sixty years of age, who was evidently a thorough disciplinarian. He was obliging and communicative; and told me he had read with pleasure my articles on "Calcutta Charities" in our paper, and heartily endorsed every word I had written. He said a great deal more, and before I left the office showed me his discharge certificate from the Army, in which he had been a sergeant, and also his Mutiny medal. We went with him over the male ward of the almshouse. I need not describe the occupants; poor things! They all looked becomingly miserable. I think there were some Eurasians among them, but the majority were pure Europeans. Mr. McGuire—for that was the superintendent's name—asked us to stay and see them fed, as it was their dinner-hour. We saw stew being doled out of a big saucepan into small bowls and put on a table. Each bowl was taken by its owner to a long, bare table, with forms down each side, and the meal, after grace being said, commenced. I felt uneasy while watching the poor things eating as if they were animals, so made a move to the women's quarters. As we walked up the stairs to the top of the building set apart for females, Mr. McGuire called out, "Mrs. Smith!" and the matron of the place, a woman of about forty, appeared. I spoke to her but little. She showed me the women working at a table, mending or making house linen, and also their rooms. The inmates themselves took small notice of me: they looked bored and sad, evidently remembering that visitors who give them no substantial help, but who beam on them with a patronizing smile, are in these parts as common as they are useless. I felt that I should have liked to have spoken to the poor women, and to have asked them if I could help them in little presents of tea or other things; but Mr. McGuire seemed to have divined my wish, for he told me they live very comfortably, having everything they could reasonably wish for as paupers. The word "pauper" jarred on me, but I said nothing as I gazed sorrowfully on them. One old woman, evidently with bad sight, was trying to hem a quilt. She appeared to be working under such difficulties on account of her eye-sight that I thought a pair of spectacles might be got for her. However, she was a "pauper," and paupers are not beings to be favoured with such luxuries! I asked if I might read to them once a week, but was referred to the committee of the District Charitable Society for permission, which I applied for, but received no answer to my letter. If I had been given the least encouragement, or even sanction to have done so, I could have provided these poor women with many little comforts; but I was not. Brother John said little, but was as much struck with the defensive attitude of the officials as I was; for he was the first to speak of it on our way home.

I must here explain that Indian institutions, like the one in question, are usually presided over by Government officials, who have little time to spare from their routine work for the exhibition of sympathy and practical kindness. The climate, too, greatly militates against philanthropic efforts in the cause of unpaid duties. Hence, the tendency to shift the *onus* of superintendence on subordinates, whose actions their superiors have to support, or to burden themselves with a large amount of personal attendance. With such an alternative, the choice generally accepted can easily be guessed. As long as things go outwardly smoothly, the subordinate draws his salary, plays the vicarious part of big man, and no doubt enjoys the well understood perquisites of such offices. If a public *exposé* takes place, the high official gets worried and questioned about a subject with which he has failed to keep himself in touch; the subordinate sees with dismay the chances of his direct and indirect emoluments being snatched from his grasp. Hence, the entire staff bitterly resent any journalistic comments on their working that are not wholly laudatory. All such officials, therefore, act on the principle of *L'état, c'est moi*. "If" say they, "you have got anything to find fault with, report it to me; but don't write to the papers." If the would-be reformer acts contrary to this dictum, he will make such officials his bitterest enemies. In such an ignoble category, men like Dr. MacLaren, superintendent of the Dehra Dun Asylum, and Mr. Ackworth and Dr. Weir, of Bombay, find no place; for their object is not to gain credit for charitable work they do not perform, but to relieve and comfort those under their kindly charge.

We were about to depart from the almshouse when I espied a number of low red-brick buildings enclosed in a small compound on the opposite side of the road. On inquiring the name of the place, I was told it was the Leper Asylum. "May I go over it?" I asked the superintendent of the almshouse. "Yes, if you are not afraid," he replied; "I am also superintendent of the Leper Asylum; but I may tell you that I have never taken a lady over the place before." I looked at Brother John, and asked him if he would prefer to wait for us outside, or go into the abode of leprosy. He said he would like to accompany us; so we all went. I had frequently seen and pitied lepers in the streets; but had never before been brought into communication with them.

The illustration facing this page will give my readers an idea of the leper, as he is to be seen in the Indian public thoroughfares. We throw the poor things a few coppers in passing; but, as there are no lepers in England, the majority of us know little about the horrible disease from which they suffer, and are therefore inclined to regard them as ordinary beggars. I had read "Life and Letters of Father Damien," and from that little book, which was lent me by the nuns of the Lorretto Convent in Calcutta, I learned something of leprosy; just enough perhaps to make me wish to know more and to see for myself what was the condition of the sufferers.

We were taken into an enclosure bounded by a high wall, and containing three long, one-storied, detached brick buildings, which, I was informed, were for the female lepers, and that there were three similar buildings on the other side of the compound, separated by a wall, for the men. As I walked up a few steps which raised the building from the level of the road, and entered the first ward, I was conscious of a "faint" smell (which is peculiar to the disease) emanating from it. We entered a long room with a

A LEPER BEGGAR.

[*p.* 12.

stone floor, and rows of beds ranged down each side. Lying or sitting on these beds—for there was not a vestige of any other kind of furniture—were several native women, all more or less bandaged. They looked up at me with a pitifully sad expression on their faces. One woman tore off her bandages and exposed a few diseased stumps remaining from what had once been fingers. The smell in the place was very bad; the sheets on the beds were discoloured and dirty; the bandages covering the sores of these poor wretches were filthy. I would fain have spoken a few words of comfort to them, for my heart was sad within me; but knowing very little of the language, I could do no more than make a few friendly gestures. Brother John told them we should come again, and we were just turning to depart when the superintendent said, "You haven't seen Bridget." On saying this, he lifted a filthy sheet that was tied on to a stick placed across an opening at the further end of the building, which contained a small room, or alcove, and disclosed a white woman sleeping! I was horrified to find a European woman in the Leper Asylum, and with nothing more than a dirty sheet dividing her from natives. The poor old thing, who had grey hair, was sleeping so peacefully that I begged the man not to disturb her. When we got outside I asked who she was, and found that she was an Irishwoman who had been an inmate of the asylum for many years.

The next ward we visited was constructed on exactly the same lines. In this there were, I think, seven women. The superintendent had a deal to say of a girl called Bella, who, he told us, had been studying medicine at the Umritzar Medical Mission when the disease broke out in her. Poor Bella lay on a dirty bed, and smiled feebly as we approached. Her fingers and toes were in a terrible state. The former had been dressed with something black that looked like tar. She wore no bandages on them, and there were great holes in her poor fingers, as though some wild animal had been biting pieces of flesh from them. Bella was a Eurasian, so spoke English. I could have cried aloud as I stood gazing helplessly on this young girl, cut down in the very flower of her youth, and doomed to spend the remainder of her days in this horrible abode of disease and death. "Oh, can nothing be done for her?" I asked. "Nothing," replied the superintendent; "I will give her three years to live—three years at the outside." I felt sorry that my question should have called forth such a reply; for poor Bella heard it in sad silence. I longed to comfort her, but I could think of nothing to say; it was all so horrible. I determined, however, that as no woman regularly visited the place, I would do so myself. I did not fear the disease; I only felt wretched on seeing its poor victims. I turned and spoke to another woman in European dress. She was a Polish Jewess, and was evidently afflicted with a different kind of leprosy, for her skin was the colour of indigo, and was much puffed and swollen, though no open sores were visible on her. She told me that she was married and the mother of a family. She could in no way account for her present state. When leprosy first showed itself on her, her husband cast her adrift, and refused to see or help her in any way. She had saved a little money and had been to doctors in Austria and Germany, and had tried all sorts of pretended cures, but without success. " Have you any money now?" I asked. "Yes," she replied, "I have a hundred and fifty rupees [about ten guineas] in the bank; but I would sooner starve than touch it. I am a pauper in this place; but after death I will be again a lady. The money is for my funeral; I will be buried in my own coffin, as a Jewess." I asked them if they would like some books to read, but they shook their heads sadly, and said that their sight was going fast, and reading hurt their eyes too much. They tried to speak cheerfully; but it was all terribly sad. Brother John could hardly trust himself to speak to poor Bella, while she herself seemed ready to cry. I looked at the miserable bareness of the place, and at the native women squatting about on the floor, and inquired if they had no chairs or washstands, or any more furniture than what I saw. They shook their heads. The Jewess pointed to a little oil-stove that was worn out and full of holes, and asked me if I would try to get her a new one, as she had no stove to boil water for her tea. I found that they washed themselves at a tap in the enclosure, but had neither bath-tubs or washstands. The sheets on their beds were supposed to be changed once a week: it was evident from their colour that they could not have been washed oftener. I wish to lay particular stress on the need there was of clean bed-linen and underclothing, both from the offensive nature of the disease and from the tropical heat of the climate. In the alcove attached to this ward we found another girl, called Daisy, whom the superintendent informed me was of Scotch parentage, but who had been suckled as an infant by a Madrassi nurse, who had afterwards turned out to be a leper. Her features were terribly distorted by the disease. Her fingers and toes were in much the same state as those of poor Bella, and she wore a green shade over her eyes. There were a couple of wicker chairs in her little room, also an accordion, with which the superintendent told me she used to accompany herself to songs; that she had a sweet voice, and often sang to the other lepers. "To whom do these women apply for their wants?" I asked. "To me," said Mr. McGuire. "I come here once a week." "But is there no woman to look after such things?" "No," he said; "women don't care to come to such places as these." I passed sorrowfully out, telling Daisy and the others that I would soon return with fruit, flowers, etc., which they said they would like. They smiled sadly, as though doubting my word, having had, as I afterwards discovered, many other promises of the kind which had not been kept. Poor Bella was tortured by flies, which surrounded her open sores in swarms. The smell, too, of the disease was so great that I was perforce obliged to walk with my handkerchief to my face the whole time. It was a very hot day, and I felt bitterly sorry for these poor sufferers, without fans, lavender water, or any little comforts whatever. I would fain have fled from this pestilent abode, and yet I lingered, wishing in my helplessness that I had the power of God behind me to enable me to say to these poor women, " I will, be thou clean." As it was, I could only stand gazing sadly on them, wondering why God had so afflicted His creatures. I walked as one bewildered through another ward, wherein were nine miserable native women, all more or less terrible to behold. " Is there no English doctor to attend to the European women here? " I asked. " No," replied the superintendent. " There is a native doctor, at a salary of twenty rupees a month." " How many lepers are there? " " Seventy-six." " But you have not half of the lepers in Calcutta in the asylum? " "Half! Why we only touch the fringe of leprosy." "Has Government done nothing in the matter?" "So far, no, though an inquiry is to be made some day with a view to providing accommodation for lepers." "Are they allowed to go in and out of the asylum when they like?" "There is no law to prevent them," he replied. "A leper falls fainting by the way-side, he is seized by the police, and conveyed in a third-class hackney carriage to the asylum. As soon as he has had his wounds dressed, has gained a little strength, and finds himself able to do so, he walks out into the streets again to beg. The Europeans do not go out."

He then asked us if we would like to see the men, and, on our replying that we would, conducted us to the opposite side of the grounds, through a door labelled "Male Ward," and into three buildings exactly similar to those we had just quitted. We walked down the first ward, filled with poor diseased specimens of humanity, in silence. The heat and smell of the place, and the filthy sheets and flies surrounding these poor lepers, were a sight that I shall never, never forget. One poor, half-naked creature was sitting in a corner trying to adjust a bandage round his legs, which, with only one or two stumps in the place of fingers, was to him no easy task. My first impulse was to fix the dirty rag for him; but I suddenly remembered that contact with this terrible disease might possibly be fatal to me, so passed on. In the next ward, which was even in a dirtier state than any that I had previously visited, the native lepers were crowded together as thickly as possible. A horrible smell pervaded the place. Bits of dirty stained bandages hung here and there. On the floor, curled up on a piece of Indian matting, lay the form of a man in the last stage of leprosy. His back was turned to me, and, although I spoke a word to him, he made no sign, no movement. I stood and looked at him in his misery. His poor bones were almost protruding through his skin, which was drawn over his body like parchment. He groaned aloud, as if in agony, every now and then moistening his parched lips with his tongue. There was no friend or attendant near to give him a drop of water. All his fellow-sufferers in the wards seemed to be watching for the end. I asked if water could be given him, but was told that he had better be left to die in peace. He was a native, and men of his caste will not, I believe, accept a drink of water from a

European's hands, or from a European water vessel: I know not whether the agonies he was enduring would have induced him to break his caste. Poor wretch, he carried our heartfelt sympathy with him on his journey into the unknown country, as well as our will to have helped him if we could have done so in any way. He died, I was told, a few hours after we left the asylum. About sixpence in coppers had been found on him, which sum was duly handed over to the authorities, who buried him according to the custom of his race.

There were three English-speaking Eurasian lepers in this ward. One man enlisted my sympathies on his behalf about some property which was confiscated to the State on the death of his mother, but which he asserts virtually belonged to him. He had made a struggle to retain possession of it, and had addressed a long petition to Lord Dufferin, who was then Viceroy of India; but, having failed to prove his legitimacy, was informed that nothing could possibly be done for him. I found him a refined, well-educated man, very fond of reading George Eliot's works, and any well written novels.

The others are two Eurasian lads who are

cousins. One about 22, the other 10 years of age. I felt much sympathy for the poor child, cut off from everyone, and doomed to spend what should be his brightest days in this awful place. He is a nice-looking boy, with a bright face, and a sweet, kindly disposition; and is devoted to drawing and painting, which he can do remarkably well. He has often since drawn dogs, cows, and different animals, and laid them out on his bed for me to see and admire. Indeed, so well were some of these executed that I should have liked to have shown them to friends of mine, had it been safe to have handled them. Leprosy was only just asserting itself on him; no sores were visible, but his fingers were doubled up, and a few ominous spots were on his body. His cousin is a leper in a more advanced stage, so one would be led to infer from this that the disease has been transmitted by heredity. I do not know how he managed to do his drawing and painting so well as he did, for there was neither a chair or table in the ward, so he must have used the bed as a table, and worked in a kneeling position.

Brother John and I drove home from the leper asylum in silence, as our hearts were too full for words. It seemed terrible that men and women should be living in the very midst of this crowded city as in a living tomb. Women, too, of my own caste and country, left alone to die without a friend in the world. One lady, Mrs. Grant, the matron of an institution known as the Military Orphan School, at Kidderpore, had visited them occasionally; but when I first went there four months had elapsed without their seeing her. This, I am certain, was no fault of hers; as she has many other duties to perform, and the Indian climate seldom allows one to continue well for any lengthened period. The men, poor things! had had no visitor to practically help them. Mr. Hall, the clergyman of the district, was in the habit of reading prayers in the little church attached to the Leper Asylum on certain Sundays; but the lepers did not appreciate mere words. His wife, Mrs. Hall, took to visiting the native leper women after I had published articles in our paper, and after I had raised a substantial fund for the cause I had at heart; but, though she would distribute flowers to the natives, she always refrained from giving any to the European and Eurasian women, who would have greatly appreciated such presents.

CHAPTER III.

THE ACCOUNT I WROTE—BRIDGET—AN OFFICIAL VISIT TO THE LEPERS.

WHEN I arrived home from the asylum, I went at once to find my husband, to tell him all that I had seen, and ask him to help me in doing something for the lepers. He was out, unfortunately, and, no one else being in the house, I tried to interest my little boy in the fate of the poor leper child whom I had just seen. His baby brain could not grasp the full extent of my meaning; but he understood enough to offer his scrap-book and promise me his musical-box and other things, all of which were duly handed over to the poor little leper next day.

I could do nothing all day but brood over what I had seen. In the evening, with the incidents fresh on my mind, I sat down and wrote an account of them for our paper. This raised for me the anger of the officials in charge of the place, who had accepted the responsibility of caring for the lepers. I described exactly what I saw and smelt. If I had not written the truth, Brother John, who was with me, would have corrected my statements when appealed to in the matter, instead of publicly corroborating them, as he afterwards did. My husband thoroughly entered into, and appreciated, my wish to relieve the sufferers, and we presented ourselves next day at the asylum with offerings of fruit, flowers, fans, scent, biscuits, jam, clean linen for bandages, sheets, underclothing, and as many other things as I could think of. These things were tearfully received by the poor women, including Bridget, whom I now had an opportunity of seeing for the first time. Mr. McGuire was not pleased with me. He said they had all they required, and informed me, when I told the women I should try and get sufficient money to allow them a rupee a week each for extra washing, etc., that the Jewess had money in the bank, and that my money was not required. I happened to know about this money, and the use for what it was being kept, so allowed his remarks to pass in silence. Bridget was a strange and weird sight when I first saw her. She wore a short black petticoat, reaching a little below her knees, and a soiled cotton jacket that had once been white. She had evidently gone without a bath for a long time, for her face and neck were dirty. Her bare feet were swollen, but there were no leprous sores on her, nor any distortion of her fingers or toes. As she stood towering above me, a tall, gaunt, starved-looking woman, I noticed a wild, restless look in her eyes which appeared to me to be a sort of challenge. On a table near her were some old loaves of bread from which all the crumb had been eaten, leaving nothing but the outside crust, that, from want of teeth, she had been unable to eat. There was also a little sour milk in a bowl. I inquired and found that her diet was bread, milk and a little coarse sugar, and that she begged scraps of curry, or *dall* (lentil) and rice from the inmates. It appears that at the Calcutta Leper Asylum there is a milk diet, on which Bridget was placed, and which consisted of twenty-two ounces of bread and a quart of milk daily, and a little sugar, and a meat diet;

the latter being sufficient for an adult, but the former was not. Bridget had her choice of the two diets, and, as she was loth to sacrifice her milk, which she would have to do if she chose the meat diet, elected to take the milk diet. The rules of the place were not sufficiently elastic to admit of a milk diet varied with meat. Bridget, therefore, in order to keep body and soul together, was obliged to beg food from the other inmates. She replied, when I asked her why she had not taken a bath, that there was no place in which she could bathe. Outside, there was a brick building that had evidently been constructed for the use of native women, and without reference to the requirements of Europeans. This building was divided into three small compartments, in each of which there was a tap for water and a drain for its outlet. There were no doors of any kind. I must here explain that the tap, rather than the more convenient bathing-tub, was selected in the interests of sanitation. The floor was of stone or concrete, and the wall in front, which shut off the bathing compartments from view, was open at both ends. My lady readers will understand how repugnant it is to the feelings of white women to bathe in a place in which they are not entirely secure from observation, even from that of their own sex ; a condition which is not obtainable at the Calcutta Leper Asylum. Bridget, having been brought up in Ireland with some ideas of decency, would not take a bath under these conditions ; so went without.

After making this discovery, I could not rest until I had written a letter to Mr. Lambert, the Commissioner of Police, asking for an interview. He granted my request, and appointed a time for me to call at his office. I found him a typical official, the performance of whose routine duties allowed him but little scope for the exercise of personal sympathy. I told him of the state of the Leper Asylum exactly as I had found it. He gave me little satisfaction, but ended by remarking that he and Mr. Justice Prinsep, who was President of the District Charitable Society, were going down to the Leper Asylum on the following morning, and that he would be glad if I would then shew them the dirty sheets described in my article which had appeared in our paper. I was too much awed by Mr. Lambert's official manner to point out to him the futility of such a quest; for the most rigid believer in the artlessness of human nature would have known that the sheets destined to meet the forthcoming scrutiny, after all that had been written and read about their previous state, would be characterised, as far as possible, by scrupulous purity. However, being in a position to be thankful for the smallest mercy, I accepted Mr. Lambert's offer, and drove down to the asylum, with my husband, on the following morning. Mr. Prinsep, who, I believe, had never been to the place before, appeared to be amused on seeing me, and was little inclined to treat the inquiry seriously. Owing to my article, no doubt, the asylum had undergone a thorough cleaning; the sheets were clean, and the place tidied up. Mr. Lambert, without a smile on his face, turned to us and said that he failed to see any cause for complaint, and that the place was clean. At that moment I saw a dying leper lying on a filthy bed, the sheets of which were covered with spots of blood and matter. I pointed this out to Mr. Lambert, who asked the man how often his sheets were changed. "We have a clean sheet every eight or nine days," replied the man in English. I had given the time as once a week in our paper, so it was even longer than I had stated. When we got outside, Mr. Prinsep joined us, and we went to Bridget's room. I asked Mr. Prinsep if he considered 22 ounces of bread, a quart of thin milk, and 4 ounces of coarse sugar a day sufficient for her? He turned to me and said he certainly thought it plenty. I could not help looking at his portly and well-nourished form, and comparing it with that of the thin, starved-looking old Irishwoman, standing at the door and offering a bowl of well-watered milk for his inspection.

My readers may imagine that in the face of so much opposition, I was beginning to lose heart. While these persons were inspecting the tank in which the lepers' clothes were washed, I went into Daisy's room, and gathering the three English-speaking lepers—Bella, Daisy, and the Jewess—around me, I begged of them to speak out and tell these gentlemen of their need of a female attendant, of washstands, and a place in which they could bathe in private, as well as of the bad food of which they had complained to me. The poor things said they would, but when the three stern men stood

AN OFFICIAL VISIT.

before them, and Mr. Lambert asked, in his severest police tones, what complaints they had to make, the miserable leper women crouched down on the floor and were silent! What "complaints" dared they make? Did they not know that such men possessed the power of turning them, diseased and penniless as they were, into the streets at any moment? The horror and disgrace of a European leper woman begging in the streets was an idea that they could never have tolerated—anything rather than that. There is a certain amount of sympathy accorded to native lepers, but Europeans afflicted in like manner are regarded more as wild beasts than as human beings. Could they have uttered a word of complaint under the circumstances? Of course not. To me, as an Englishwoman, the sight of these three leper women, cowering before the very men who posed before the world as their friends and benefactors, was one that roused every feeling within me to rebellion! However, after all, I was only regarded as a meddlesome unit, whose blame or praise was a matter of utter indifference to persons of position and standing; though who knows but that a merciful God in Heaven, the Father of the fatherless and afflicted, to whom all hearts are opened, did not see and pass judgment on one and all of us who stood before Him that day? It may have been this thought which caused me to bridle my tongue and refrain from giving utterance to strong words. Anyhow, I did manage to control my feelings sufficiently to enable me to speak calmly to Mr. Lambert, to point out to him the bathing-place, and to ask him, as a man who had daughters of his own, if he considered it a fitting bath-room for European women. Mr. Lambert, looking into the bathing-place, saw a native woman taking her bath, and retired in confusion. I commented on the unprotected state of the European women, who were obliged to bathe in this place, which was exposed in an enclosure where native male dressers, washermen, cooks and others were in the habit of walking, and suggested the desirability of having a door placed in one of the bathing partitions, which should be supplied with a bathing-tub, and reserved for the use of European women, who are unaccustomed to bathing like natives. I was informed that such additions were altogether superfluous, and that if the ends of the outer wall were rounded or curved in, instead of being straight as they then were, all requirements as to the privacy and comfort of the bathing arrangements would then be met. This was done, but up to the time of writing, no door or bath-tub has been provided for the use of Daisy, Bella, or the Jewess, who have to make their daily ablutions under the tap as best they can. I may mention that there were no arrangements at all in this asylum for giving the patients a warm bath.

CHAPTER IV.

NEWSPAPER CRITICISM—"TRUTH" AND MR. PRINSEP—
"THE QUEEN."

As I have already mentioned, the remarks I wrote about the Calcutta Leper Asylum made the honorary officials of that institution "mad" at being "shown up" (which was a necessary consequence of the appearance of a true account of that institution) as mere *poseurs*, and not as workers, as they fain would have appeared before the Government from whom they received pay, and expected preferment. Being the head of the institution, and never having visited it, to my knowledge, except on the occasion of the official visit I have described in the previous chapter, Mr. Prinsep was, of course, my bitterest opponent. Consequently appeared the following extract in *Truth* of the 10th of July last year :—

On May 15th reference was made in *Truth* to a deplorable account of the Leper Asylum, Calcutta, given by Mrs. Alice Hayes, in a local paper called *Hayes' Sporting News*. I have now received from Mr. Justice Prinsep, president of the District Charitable Society, which has the control of the Asylum in question, a letter in which the writer states that the statements in *Hayes' Sporting News* "are absolutely without foundation, and are merely the careless and inaccurate reports of a hysterical, irresponsible woman seeking for notoriety." Mr. Justice Prinsep does not deal with the whole of the statements specifically, but he states (1) that in only one of the six buildings " can it be pretended that there is any overcrowding at all;" (2) " that the medical attendance is appropriate ; " (3) " that a person referred to by Mrs. Hayes as a native doctor is the ' compounder ;' " and (4) that he could, if it were worth while, "similarly refute all Mrs. Hayes's statements." He also sends me a copy of a letter addressed on behalf of the management to the local press ; but I find here quite as much admission of the impeachment as denial. I find further that in subsequent articles in *Hayes' Sporting News*, Mrs. Hayes adheres to her original statements, and points out that many of them are unanswered or unanswerable. It is impossible for me at this distance of time and space to go further into the matter, but the impression left on my mind is that Mr. Justice Prinsep's abusive language of Mrs. Hayes is entirely unjustified, and that this Leper Asylum will probably be all the better for the light that has been turned on it.

Mr. Prinsep, being a lawyer (he was Judge in the Calcutta High Court), was well acquainted with the old legal maxim : "when you have got no case, abuse the other side." Consequently his strong language—

however unbecoming it was in a man of his high official position, and addressed to a woman—was a convincing proof that the words I had written were true. His assertion that I made a mistake in the designation of the medical attendant, proves how sorely he was pressed to find something to refute; for the fact of a "compounder" being lower in grade than a "native doctor" made my case all the stronger.

I received not only a kindly pat on the back from Mr. Labouchere; but a most sympathetic article under the heading, " A Lady's Work Among the Lepers," appeared on the 22nd of the following November in *The Queen*, as follows :—

A Calcutta correspondent writes :—"Perhaps your readers may be interested to hear what a woman has done for the lepers in the Calcutta Leper Asylum. Mrs. Alice Hayes, lady correspondent of a local weekly entitled *Hayes' Sporting News*, edited by her husband Captain Horace Hayes, lately commenced writing in her husband's paper a series of articles on Calcutta Charities, visiting each one for this purpose, amongst them the Calcutta Leper Asylum. She found entombed there about seventy lepers—men and women, and one or two children. Amongst the inmates are some Eurasian and European men and women. The latter seem, from Mrs. Hayes' accounts, to be badly furnished with the comforts of life. Two of the women had been students in some of our large public schools before the disease showed itself, and were hidden away here by parents and friends anxious to put such a visitation from the world's gaze. Mrs. Hayes was much touched at the sad loneliness of these poor creatures, and describes their condition most vividly in the paper before mentioned, inviting the help of the public to form a small fund to provide them with small creature comforts which the asylum had omitted to supply, such as sufficient clothes, sheets, washstands, fruit, jam, illustrated papers, &c., and proposing personally to visit the asylum weekly, and distribute amongst the afflicted people the small offerings. Her appeal has been very generously responded to, and money, clothing, etc., have been sent to her. Nobly too, does she, week after week fulfil her self-imposed mission, going among these poor outcasts, and cheering their loneliness with sprightly talk and news of the outside world, and leaving each time some memento of her kindly presence. Leprosy in our tropical climate assumes its most loathsome aspect, and many of the inhabitants of our Leper Asylum are in a very advanced stage of the disease. The sight, as described by others whom curiosity or pity perhaps has tempted there, is enough to appal any man. I hardly think a second visit is paid, however good the intention of doing so. Mrs. Hayes, on the contrary, as I have said before, has never failed a single Tuesday to visit her poor suffering fellow-creatures. We read with admiration of the deeds of Florence Nightingale, Sister Dora, Sister Gertrude, and I think we should add to this list the name of our brave young citizen, Mrs. Alice Hayes, whose kindness and courage are certainly unequalled in India."

I had a great deal of criticism in the Indian papers. The Calcutta ones, which are largely dependent on the support of the local officials, chiefly backed up the principle that the king can do no wrong; while the journals that were free from Calcutta official influence, as a rule, took my side. The result, however, was favourable; for subscriptions from all parts of India came to our fund, which, since our departure from the East, has, I am very sorry to say, decreased. As I can now no longer personally stimulate support, I am doing the next best thing by writing this book.

CHAPTER V.

EFFORTS TO COMFORT—OUR SUBSCRIPTION FUND—IMPROVEMENTS.

I MANAGED, after a deal of trouble, to give each of the leper women a small tin-enamelled washstand; but much opposition was brought to bear on me by the officials in my efforts to alleviate their sufferings in any way. Daisy, who spoke to me about the bathroom, says she hangs up a towel in front of the doorway and so secures privacy in that way; but it is a wretched makeshift at the best. Seeing that no female attendant was provided to attend to the personal requirements of these poor women, whose disease renders them miserably helpless, we thought out a project by which a native woman could be got to wait on them.

By this time my article, which, as I explained, had been written when the scene presented to me on my first visit to the Leper Asylum was fresh and vivid in my recollection, had been published in our paper and had been productive of good results. Parcels of linen, books, soap, tea, and various things were sent me, together with subscriptions amounting to over Rs. 800. Out of this we sent a cheque for Rs. 192 to the committee of the District Charitable Society, with the request that a female attendant be provided for the female European and Eurasian inmates of the Leper Asylum, at a salary of Rs. 8 a-month, for two years. This money was, I am glad to say, accepted by the committee, and the attendant procured. We read an account in a local paper of Dr. Unna's new medicine for leprosy, which had been highly recommended by Dr. Milton, senior surgeon of St. John's Hospital for Diseases of the Skin, London, and at once forwarded to the committee of the D. C. S., from our Leper Fund, a cheque for Rs. 250, with the request that the money be used in procuring the medicine from England and giving it a fair trial in the Calcutta Leper Asylum, together with a promise of a further

BROTHER JOHN.   [p. 41.

remittance of Rs. 250 for this object should it be required. This money was, after some discussion, accepted, and an order for the medicine sent to England. I must not forget to mention that we pointed out in our letter to the Committee the advisability of having the new medicine tried here by an English doctor. I had secured the confidence of the public, who sympathised with me in my work, and sent me various sums of money from time to time. Monthly subscriptions to our Leper Fund amounted to Rs. 40. With this sum I was able to spend Rs. 10 weekly on comforts for the white female lepers. I gave the four of them a rupee each, and spent the remaining six rupees on jam, fruit, biscuits, lavender water, flowers, etc., always reserving a few rupees, which I exchanged into coppers, and gave each native leper woman as many as I could afford. My weekly visits to the Leper Asylum were always paid in company with Brother John, who arranged to go with me every Tuesday, and who was my most staunch and sincere helper in this work. We had at first to encounter much opposition from the officials; were not allowed to visit the asylum without sending for the superintendent, nor permitted to give anything to the lepers without first having our gifts pass through his hands. I found this arrangement most unpleasant, for among my gifts to these poor friendless women were things that are not generally allowed to pass through the hands of a man, and, besides, I often wanted to speak to the women alone, and the presence of the superintendent was in no way desirable. Being utterly powerless to move the men on the Committee, who regarded me as an enemy to be thwarted at every turn, and held up to scorn and ridicule, I appealed to the public through our paper, with the result that several indignant letters from sympathisers appeared in the local daily papers. This caused a change of front. Mrs. Smith, the matron at the almshouse, opposite the asylum, was told to attend me in my visits, and distribute the gifts I took to the lepers. I noticed, also, that some improvements had been made in the asylum. Bridget's room had been cut off entirely from the native ward by a wooden partition; a bath-room, constructed of matting and bamboos, for her special use, had been fitted up in the small verandah at the back of her room. The food of the lepers had also been undergoing a change, and Bridget was given a little curry and rice, in addition to her bread and milk. The people who are always ready to put an entirely false construction on the motives of others had been busy with their tongues, and had told Bridget and the others that I had only taken them up as a "fad," to drop as quickly when I got tired of them. This was all duly repeated to me by the lepers themselves, who had begun to put by their weekly rupee against the time when supplies would be stopped. Of course, I was hurt and grieved to think that people could be so ungenerous as to say such things to the poor lepers, and tried to impress on Bridget that so long as I remained in Calcutta, with health and strength, I would let nothing prevent me from paying my weekly visit to them, and that when I was unable to do so, failing any lady, Brother John had promised to take up the work. This satisfied the old woman somewhat. She considered for a time, and then said, "Yes, I think you are telling the truth, because you have always kept your promises. I asked Mrs. —— to bring me some red herrings, and she said she would; but they never came.

When I asked you, you brought them. Besides, a young clergyman came here once—only once—and promised to send me some picture-books, but he never sent them; so you see we haven't much faith in people now: we only believe them when we see them keep their promises." I often used to find Daisy, the Jewess, and Bella together in Daisy's little room, talking of their affliction. Suffering and sorrow have bound at least two of these women together in the holiest ties of friendship and love. One day I found them much depressed. I know not what had happened: I think there had been trouble with the officials. Whatever it was, they were afraid to tell me more than that they had been forbidden to speak about their feeding and treatment, as I had been publishing articles on their state in our paper. When I told them that money had been sent to England for the newly-recommended medicine for them, they were delighted; asked me many questions as to what it was like, when it would arrive, whether I thought it would do them any good, and many others that I was unable to answer.

To show the horrible neglect, as far as medical

attention was concerned, that existed in this Leper Asylum, I may mention that the patients were in charge of a native "compounder" (see Mr. Prinsep's remark on page 35). Although Bridget, the old Irishwoman, was regarded by the officials of the Asylum as a leper, my husband and I doubted the accuracy of their judgment in this case; for it seemed impossible that she could be in such fair health, as she was, had she been thus afflicted for a dozen or more years, as they asserted. Her features were as regular and clean cut, as they would be in any woman of her age; and were free, as far as we could see, from any tubercles or nodules peculiar to leprosy, especially when it is of long standing. There was no distortion of her fingers or toes (she generally went about barefoot), and there was no staining of the skin of the uncovered parts of her body. Her feet and lower parts of her legs were somewhat swollen, which condition might very easily have been induced by debility brought on by the insufficiency of the food she was allowed, by the effects of the enervating climate, by want of proper exercise, and by age. She suffered from no leprous pains, the acuteness of her senses were in no way diminished, and she was affected with no special lassitude. The only symptom which in her was at all diagnostic (if I may be pardoned for using a medical term which exactly conveys my meaning) of leprosy was a feeling of numbness which she had. My husband, who is a Fellow of the Royal College of Veterinary Surgeons, and who has studied the nature of disease both in the lower animals and in man, tells me that this feeling of numbness is not peculiar to leprosy, but that it might have arisen, in Bridget, from another and not very dissimilar disease, which Bridget, according to the Leper Asylum officials, had contracted many years ago. I may also mention that this poor Irishwoman was entirely free from the peculiar odour which Dr. MacLaren (than whom there is no more experienced authority) regards (see page 116) as diagnostic of leprosy. Besides, Mrs. Grant, who had taken an interest in Bridget for many years, told us that Dr. Kenneth Stewart, who was formerly in practice in Calcutta, and who had examined Bridget, had told her that the Irishwoman was not a leper. As we had only the unprofessional opinion of the Asylum people against our contention, and as we thought it horrible that on such slight evidence this poor creature should be stowed away in a native leper asylum, we applied and received permission to have her examined by Dr. Crombie, superintendent of the Calcutta General Hospital. This was done, and Dr. Crombie gave it his opinion that she was a leper, because of the numbness or *anæsthesia* (see page 116) from which she suffered.

CHAPTER VI.

MISS O'BRIEN—AMATEUR ACTORS—A PERFORMANCE IN AID OF OUR FUND.

ALL this time I was doing little or nothing for the male lepers. My monthly subscriptions were not sufficient to allow of my extending any gifts to them, much as I should have liked to have done so. Brother John undertook to provide them with tobacco, but he could do no more; for his salary amounted to but Rs. 50 (about £3 10s.) a month, out of which he had to keep himself and to feed many hungry sailors who found their way to his rooms. The native women, too, in the other wards were asking me to bring them fruit. Feeling myself cramped from want of funds, I took counsel with a dear friend of mine, Miss O'Brien, who lived opposite our house, and who had assisted me in many ways with my work. She was the eldest of a large family, who were left almost penniless on the death of their father. Instead of asking alms of friends and acquaintances, she opened a school for young children, and by dint of hard and constant work, managed to support and assist the whole family until they were able to work for themselves. Another sister is the possessor of a fine soprano voice, which was trained in England by Signor Visetti. She is now one of the most popular singing-mistresses in Calcutta, and is able to assist her elder sister in keeping their old mother in comfort. These two admirable girls became greatly interested in my work among the lepers. The elder one read my articles to the school children. Over a hundred scholars were told of Bella and Daisy in the Leper Asylum. They raised a subscription among themselves, and sent me various small sums from time to time. The school-mistress, being cleverer than I am at book-keeping, took charge of my subscription-book and fund-money, giving me what I required every week for the lepers. She would have liked to have accompanied me on one of my visits to the asylum, but her mother forbad her doing so, which, considering her position as head of a large school, was perhaps wise. Finding our Leper Fund getting low, and myself unable to do anything for the male lepers, my friends and I put our heads together one Sunday afternoon, and wrote out an appeal for more money, which we had printed and distributed round Calcutta. We also thought out a programme for an entertainment to be given in aid of the Leper Fund, to which we would all contribute help. I suggested that a lady pianiste should play a solo, my friend should sing something, we would ask a couple of gentlemen friends to sing also, the school children could wind up the first part with the pretty Highland schottische they had danced in the theatre on their last prize distribution day, and that I would arrange for the acting of " Our Bitterest Foe," a pretty little play for three actors, which would fill the second part of the programme. Alas! the getting up of any performance is not at all so easy as it seems. Mrs. De Montmorency Smith will not promise to take part in any concert without first having had the names of the other performers submitted for her approval.

Then Miss de Courcy Jones will not perform unless she can choose her own place on the programme. The men, I must say, generally behave better. Having promised their help in the good cause of charity, they do not often worry one with petty tricks. Our proposed play was a difficult one to cast. Those of my readers who have seen it performed in England will remember that each of the three characters requires a deal of sound, strong acting. I had helpers in plenty; for amateur actors of a sort are not scarce in India; but they were not the right kind. Strange it is that almost every amateur actor is a low-comedy man! Our first rehearsal was altogether ridiculous. The man who essayed the part of the dignified Prussian General, Von Rosenberg, considered it the correct thing to sit in the presence of a lady with his feet on a chair! I had arranged my drawing-room as a stage, and had put each chair in its place, so, of course, could not allow the General to upset everything. When I told him of it, he answered stiffly, "That he wanted to make the part as natural as possible, and that men, when taking their ease, *do* sit in that position." Knowing that a play cannot succeed, if each actor is allowed to adopt what "business" he pleases, I told him that Mr. John McLean had taught me his way of playing the piece, and that I should prefer it done according to his instructions. My General removed his feet from the chair with an angry grunt. I discovered that he stammered on occasions of excitement, and when he looked at me and commenced his first speech, saying, "You are s-s-s-s-s—ad, Mademoiselle?" my other actor, who was to play the part of Henri de la Fere, and who was listening behind a screen, burst into such a fit of laughter that we were unable to proceed for some time. On hearing this, the General got up from his chair and walked up and down the stage in long strides, calling out to Henri to come and play the part himself, if he could do it better. He cooled down after a time and we were able to resume. When he came to the lines, "I am a Prussian, Mademoiselle," he emphasized the word "Prussian" by banging his fist down on the table with so much violence, that I, who was sitting on the opposite side following his speeches with the book, was startled and dropped it. This provoked repeated roars of laughter from

Henri, which so incensed the General that he refused to say another word. I did not press him to do so; for I saw that his acting would not pass muster; so we partook of afternoon tea and passed things off pleasantly with some music. When the amateurs had gone, I decided to abandon my idea of a play and have a concert only, and to engage the Calcutta Town Hall for the occasion.

I found I had many kind friends to help me in getting up my concert. Besides the performers, who gladly offered their services free of all charge, was Mr. George, a clever artist, who was at that time engaged on an illustrated paper called *The Empress*, and who designed the programmes for me; Messrs. Thacker, Spink and Co., who provided and printed them free of charge; the Great Eastern Hotel Company, who sent their workmen with flags and drapery to decorate the Town Hall; and a number of other good people who all helped to make the evening a success. The Volunteer band, under Herr Kuhlmey, played during the interval, and also after the concert. Brother John and I had a hard day's work before us in arranging the stage and decorating it with flowers and fairy lamps.

He procured a quantity of evergreens, and between us we managed to make the stage look very well. He had a large model of a ship that had been made by the sailors, and of which he was justly proud, arranged among the flags and flowers in the centre of the stage where the audience could see and admire it to their heart's content. Brother John and my husband took the tickets and showed the people into their seats. The concert was a success in every way. Mrs. Bushby, a silver medalist, and one of the best pianists in India, played the accompaniments. The soloists were Miss O'Brien, Miss Stuart, Mrs. Turnbull, Mr. Eastly, Mr. Hartland, and Father Hopkins, all well-known amateurs of Calcutta. I recited two pieces, and received a very hearty greeting from the crowded audience when I went on the stage. I thought that after all the hostilities we had encountered in connection with this leper question, that I should have a small house; but though none of the officials connected with the Leper Asylum or their friends were present at our concert, so many other people came that we had to provide more chairs to meet them all, and the Town Hall was quite full. I plucked up courage on seeing this, and recited in my very best style, gaining a hearty encore from my audience, who seemed to be thoroughly pleased with what I did. Miss O'Brien was, of course, the *prima donna* of the evening, and all the other performers were most successful with their songs.

CHAPTER VII.

WHITE LEPERS—DR. MACLAREN—HEAT AND MISERY.

Since my first visit to the Asylum two other men had been admitted, both Europeans. One man is English and was employed on the railway. He managed with the weekly rupee I was able to give him, to obtain some special kind of medicine which, he says, is doing him a deal of good. He showed me some in a small tin box. It looked like tobacco leaves and has a peculiar smell. He makes it into pills and takes several every day. There are many hundreds of different quack medicines which are advertised as "cures" for leprosy, but I have little faith in any of them. This English leper is entirely destitute, and is at the moment of writing sharing a

Dr. G. G. MacLaren.

p. 57.

common ward with natives. His sole furniture consists of the bed on which he lies; not even a chair being provided for him to sit on. He has no washstand, nor any other furniture. In the next bed to him is a man of French extraction; a very bad case. Leprosy has obtained such a hold of him that I doubt whether he will live very long. He was formerly employed in the Calcutta water-works and several letters had appeared in the daily papers written by different persons who had seen him, commenting on the danger of allowing a leper to occupy this position. He was discharged shortly after the appearance of these letters, a pension being allowed him for the support of his family. I heard that he had transmitted the disease to his wife. Notwithstanding that two pure Europeans had been admitted into the male ward, not the slightest thing has been done towards making them comfortable. How differently Dr. MacLaren treats his European patients! This admirable gentleman started in 1879 a leper asylum for natives at Dehra Dun, in the north of India, where he was in practice. This institution has been supported entirely by voluntary contributions, and Dr. MacLaren has devoted as much of his time as possible to trying to master this horrible disease with the aid of all that medical science can accomplish. In this year's report of the Dehra Dun Asylum, we read, "During this year a European—the first—has been admitted to the Asylum. As, however, he does not belong to this district, and was admitted on his own urgent request, I may here make a short statement regarding him. Mr. C. W. J., who is in his forty-sixth year, was at one time in a good situation in a Government Office; but about nineteen years ago a blotch appeared on his body which in the course of a few years developed into disfiguring sores. He visited England on furlough to get what benefit he could from home treatment. After staying and receiving treatment for some time he had to return without having received the benefit which he had so confidently hoped for. Shortly after that, he was invalided out of the Service with only a gratuity; but on appealing to Government he ultimately succeeded in having a pension granted him. In July he first made application for admission; but as there was nothing in the way of accommodation for a European in the institution, I could not give him much encouragement. Ultimately, the local Government and the Superintendent of the Dun, Mr. Nujent, magnanimously provided funds wherewith suitable accommodation and furniture was provided. A small cottage, consisting of a room, bedroom, closet, and verandah in a corner of the garden, was altered, and given up for his use, and Mr. J. came here in October." My readers may learn from this that Dr. MacLaren *did* consider the requirements of a European as being entirely separate and distinct from those of natives, and arranged for suitable accommodation for the one under his charge, previous to his reception. In Calcutta this is not done, and up to the time of writing, Europeans are herding with natives in a ward entirely devoid of furniture, except a bed each. This is not from necessity or want of funds; for the District Charitable Society is one of the richest in Calcutta. I may here explain to those of my readers who have not lived abroad that, however poor and miserably afflicted a European man or woman may be, the one possession to which they cling, and on which they hang their last shred of personal pride when everything else in the world has left them, is their nationality. Hence, they bitterly resent in their hearts, even when they are too stricken down to give vent to their feelings in words, any attempt to class them on a common footing with natives. The same commendable spirit animated St. Paul when he claimed that he was a Roman.

At this time the weather in Calcutta was intensely hot. One Tuesday, as I drove down to the Asylum, my pony, evidently overcome by the heat, staggered and seemed unable to proceed. Seeing some cabmen bathing their horses' temples with wet rags at a watering place in the road, I stopped my pony and got my native groom to do likewise to him. It revived him and we reached safely at the Asylum without further mishap. On taking up the *Statesman* newspaper next day, I read that five tramway horses had died of sunstroke about the very time that my pony became affected by the heat. The lepers at the Asylum were feeling it very much, and the smell of the disease was quite overpowering. I forwarded a gallon of phenyle for use in the Leper Asylum; but Mr. Lambert (the Commissioner of Police, who has charge of this institution) wrote across my note: "return this to Mrs. Hayes, with thanks," and the phenyle came back to me. Although some months had passed, during which time these officials were able to see for themselves that I was trying to do my best for the good of the lepers and working quietly; still they chose to maintain their hostile attitude towards me and to do their utmost to wound and annoy me in every way. Even Mr. McGuire must have felt that I was hardly treated; for, as he returned my phenyle and put it in the carriage, he showed me Mr. Lambert's letter, and assured me that he was acting under orders. Just then I heard a roar as of a number of wild animals fighting. I proceeded to the native female ward from whence it came, and saw a number of leper women all rushing at the bed on which I had placed the coppers I had counted out for each of them, and trying to get possession of the whole, tearing and going at each other like so many tigers. Mrs. Smith was able to restore order after a while; but the sight of these loathsome-looking diseased women enveloped in dirty rags and bandages trying to hurt each other for a few coppers, was one that I shall never forget. The heat was overpowering; things were all going wrong; the phenyle that Daisy had repeatedly asked for was not allowed to be given, and I returned home that day sick and wretched.

CHAPTER VIII.

NEED FOR A HOME FOR EUROPEAN AND EURASIAN LEPERS—OUR PUBLIC MEETING.

DR. WALLACE, a friend who came to lunch, on talking things over with me, proposed that instead of labouring away every week at the Government Leper Asylum under many vexatious restrictions, it would be better to try and open a Home for European and Eurasian lepers where they could find shelter and comfort, and be away from natives similarly afflicted. I entered gladly into the spirit of the proposition, but felt doubtful as to whether sufficient money would be forthcoming to carry on such an institution. We did not want it to rest on the shoulders of any one man or woman; but desired it to be properly managed by a competent committee appointed for the purpose. I was in favour of putting the proposed Home in charge of Sisters of Charity, who, the Reverend Mother Matilda of the Loretto Convent, told me, would come out from England if we could insure them a home and food, and that they would devote their lives to this holy cause. This idea was not generally approved of by my Protestant friends, who said that Catholics would be certain to want to proselytise the persons under their charge, and that, although the Sisters would devote their whole time to the care of the lepers, my subscriptions would fall off directly I placed them under any special religious body. Besides, there exists a deal of suspicious distrust of Catholics in India, which has arisen, I think, from jealousy; for it is generally, if reluctantly, conceded that Catholics manage their public charitable institutions far better than do persons of other denominations. We decided that it would be best to put Dr. Wallace's proposal to the test of public opinion, and to call a meeting at the Dalhousie Institute, which has a hall that is used for such purposes. We intended to put forward two resolutions at this meeting. The first

Female Leper.

was to show the need of such a home; for although the Government Asylum gave shelter to European and Eurasian lepers, it placed them under conditions which few of them, however sorely pressed they might be by their misery, would accept. Dr. Wallace promised to speak on this point, and to tell the audience, as he had already informed us, that he knew, from his own personal experience, of from twenty to thirty of these hapless ones who were living in their own homes in Calcutta to the danger of their friends and of the general public. Besides this score or so in the metropolis, there must be hundreds of European and Eurasian lepers scattered throughout the length and breadth of India. Only a very small proportion of these cases come before the notice of the English residents; for the relations of such lepers naturally make every possible effort to prevent the fact of the existence of the disease in their family becoming known on account of the awful ban it would lay on all the other members. I need hardly say that no one, in his or her senses, would knowingly marry into a family affected with the hereditary taint of leprosy, nor even associate on intimate terms with such comparative outcasts. Owing to the perverseness of human nature, such instances do sometimes occur. One was of a young gentleman, good-looking, well connected, charming in his manners, of great natural abilities and of irreproachable conduct, who fell in love with a young lady whose family had a trace of native blood in it, and laboured under the whispered stigma of leprosy. The young gentleman's relations used every means in their power to prevent their union, and told him distinctly that if it took place they would know him no more. Their entreaties and threats were in vain; the marriage took place; some children were born; a few years passed happily despite the alienation of his friends, and then the effects of the dire malady broke out in the young wife. The husband tried, with rare heroism, to keep a bright face on the sorrow he endeavoured to hide, and obtained the best medical advice in the world, but all in vain; for the disease went steadily on to its end in its uncheckable course. Among others in Calcutta, we knew one who regularly attended church and sat beside his fellow worshippers; a second went to meetings of the local Salvation Army and used to shake hands with the members of his religious sect; a third lived with his parents, brothers and sisters, none of whom had developed the malady; a fourth lived with his wife and family (the woman and children being apparently healthy) and eked out a precarious living by begging. We had heard of a planter, who, while we were in Calcutta, brought a brother of his, that was afflicted with leprosy, down to Calcutta with the object of placing him in the Leper Asylum; but, on seeing that it was altogether unsuitable to the requirements of a white man, he took him back with him to his own home. My husband knew an officer in the Indian Army, who was quartered in the same station with him, and who became a leper. When his condition could be no longer concealed, in the event of his going out in public, he was virtually made a prisoner of, in his house, by his friends, who screened him off from outside gaze till he died. My husband also knew of an equally sad case of a gentleman in Government employment in India, who contracted leprosy, and whose brother (his only relation in that country), as soon as he became aware of the fact, would no longer come to see him or hold any intercourse with him. Although some of his indigo planting friends, with the kindness of heart which characterises all Indian planters, used to visit him from time to time and try to cheer him up, he had to live and die with only his Native servants near him. We know of two other cases of leprosy among acquaintances of our own in India; but these are only in their first stages, and are not sufficiently advanced to prevent the sufferers from appearing in public. I may mention that the *Lancet* of the 18th July of this year (1891) reports a case of leprosy at Lisburn (Ireland) in a man who had contracted the disease at Rangoon (Burma), where he had resided ten years. There have been many other instances of Europeans contracting the disease abroad. Any destitute white man who became a leper in India would have to remain there; as the Government, very rightly, would not send him home.

What we contended and still maintain, is, that if a hospital were formed near Calcutta, or at some other convenient centre, for the reception of European and Eurasian lepers, and if it afforded a comfortable home where medical comforts and proper medical attendance were obtainable, the large majority of these poor creatures would gladly avail themselves of the opportunity of obtaining a place of rest, of receiving medical aid, and of relieving their friends of their burdensome presence. I may point out in passing, that such an asylum should, within reasonable bounds, be replete with means of making the lives of the inmates as bright as possible. While enforcing strict segregation, the patients should have ample room inside the precincts of the institution to walk about, and to engage in any harmless amusements suitable to their condition. Besides this, they should be regarded as sick people, whose ailment medicine and proper hygienic treatment can do much to relieve, even if they cannot, with our present state of knowledge, stay its course. In India, European and Eurasian leper have no such place to enter. If they go to the Calcutta Asylum, they will be treated as Natives; they will have no " medical comforts;" they will be fed in a manner unsuitable to Europeans, or to the requirements of their disease, which demands a liberal regimen; they will not be able to get a warm bath; nor will they have attendants to wash and dress them, if they be too weak or helpless to do so for themselves; they will have no grounds to walk in; they will have no means of recreation, as might be afforded by a library, a garden for them to cultivate, etc.; nor will they even have punkahs to cool the air and to keep off the flies during the intense heat of the summer; nor mosquito nets to render sleep possible at night. In making these remarks, I do not want to disparage the management of the Calcutta Leper Asylum, which is professedly intended only for the reception of Natives; but I do, most emphatically, desire to point out the pressing necessity of a hospital or asylum for European and Eurasian lepers either near Calcutta or in some other convenient centre in India, and of their being placed in a more comfortable position than they could hope to obtain in their own homes. The second resolution was for the formation of a committee, and for the discussion of ways and means to obtain the necessary funds.

On the morning fixed for the meeting, we were delighted to read in all the local papers an announcement to the effect that Government had decided to take over the lepers, and to build separate and suitable accommodation for European and Eurasian patients. This notice removed from us the burden of the undertaking we had proposed to attempt; for it would not be necessary for us to try and organise a home in the face of such an announcement. However, as we had called the meeting together, and it was then too late to postpone it or to explain matters in any other way, we decided to allow it to take place, and to simply put forward our first resolution showing the immediate want of such a home, and to let the matter rest for the present, pending the action of the Government. A few hours before the meeting took place, my husband met one of the members of the committee of the District Charitable Society, who warned him that a hostile demonstration had been prepared to nullify the effect of any resolutions brought forward by him. This gentleman informed my husband that the paid secretary of the District Charitable Society, whose father was the paid superintendent of the Leper Asylum, had sent round a circular to all whom he thought would help him, requesting them to attend our meeting and to support the counter resolutions or amendments which his party would bring forward. The initiative in this step was taken either by the secretary himself, or by someone who used him as a willing agent; for the sanction of the committee had not been obtained in taking it, nor had it been canvassed. The member of the committee in question expressed his strong sympathy with us, and regretted that his official position prevented him from according us his public support. On pointing out the extreme impropriety of the hostile action on the part of the secretary of the District Charitable Society, I may mention that he is a young Eurasian, whose social standing and personal qualifications in no way entitled him to address his employers, by circular, in the manner he did. Consequently, I conclude, that however warm and interested his feelings may have been, he acted solely and entirely from secret orders, the responsibility of which, or of an inquiry into his unauthorised conduct, rested on the President of the District Charitable Society.

The meeting came off, and the only resolution that was put forward was one to recognise the necessity for a separate Asylum or place for European and Eurasian lepers, apart from that for the Natives. My husband, who moved it, contended that as Government had decided to take up the work, we could do no more than show our readiness to help to strengthen the hands of the Government in every possible way, and to express our opinion that such an institution was sadly needed. He then informed the audience of the private circular, and appealed to his hearers if it was fair or right for men to come down to this meeting with the deliberate intention of thwarting a good work, the object of which was solely and entirely to mitigate the sufferings of the most miserable of our fellow citizens. The opposition came forward with printed amendments to controvert arguments our side had not put forward, owing to the fact that such arguments were not required now that Government had announced its intention to take up the matter. The fatal itching of speechifying was so strong on these gentlemen, that they did not see the absurdity of combatting unspoken words. Notwithstanding their eloquence and the presence of their supporters, their amendment, when put to the vote, was lost.

CHAPTER IX.

HOPE—KATE REILLY.

WHILE anxiously waiting for the action of Government, we abandoned our idea of starting the proposed home, and determined to devote the money we had previously collected in providing small comforts for the inmates of the Government Leper Asylum, whom we continued to visit every Tuesday, and to minister to their small requirements. Other lepers, who were living in Calcutta, outside of the asylum, heard of our work in it, and made a practice of coming to our house for alms. We allowed two rupees weekly to an Eurasian who was a bad leper, and who tried to keep his wife and family on what he could manage to get by begging. He had been an inmate of the Government Asylum ; but, as he found that he received there little or no medical treatment, he preferred to live outside and to procure, as far as he could afford, special treatment from a native doctor in the city. He told me he was getting much better and that he hoped soon to be cured and able again to work for his family. Hope, glorious hope, is ever present with even the most horribly afflicted of God's creatures. I have seen the distorted features of the leper man or woman brighten as though a light had been suddenly illumined within them at the mention of the word "hope"; a light that even years of suffering and disappointment was unable to extinguish.

One of the first lepers to hear of my visits to the asylum was a girl, Kate Reilly, who lived in a crowded quarter of the town, and who sent for me to go and see her. The person who came with the message looked like a respectably-dressed shopkeeper, quoted several texts from Scripture, by way, I suppose, of stimulating me into going to her friend, and wound up by telling me of all that she had done for her. When I saw Kate afterwards, she told me to come again of my own accord, and not oblige her to send Mrs. ——, who always charged her cab hire when she executed any commissions for her. I experienced some difficulty in seeing Kate when I first called. The address given me by the woman who came to my house was in a lane off Chandney Choke, one of the lowest and most thickly populated of the slums of Calcutta. It is here one may see exposed for sale everything that it is possible to imagine, from a hammer and nails or a button hook, to a complete outfit for man or horse. Side by side with legs of thin miserable-looking mutton will be seen a set of harness, gaudy and cheap; saddles that make one feel sorry for the unfortunate horse or pony on whose back they will be placed; hats and bonnets trimmed with bits of satin of the most showy colours procurable; bedsteads, tobacco, sweets, padlocks, old books, and a thousand and one miscellaneous articles repose on the benches of Chandney Choke. Drunken sailors, and soldiers, in Her Majesty's uniform, earning an honest penny by selling the Salvation Army's *War Cry*, half-caste loafers, mulattos and "shady" characters from every quarter of the globe seem to be always prowling about there in search of money or adventure. Knowing that it would be unsafe for a lady to go alone into any of these dens, I asked a gentleman friend to accompany me, and I drove as well as I could through the crowd till we came to the lane where Kate Reilly lived. Here the road was too narrow to drive along, so we alighted from the trap and walked to the house. There was a number on it, but no door, only an archway. On entering it I was conscious of the well-remembered "faint" smell of leprosy; so knew we had arrived at the right address. We passed through the archway into a small yard in which a number of Eurasian children were playing. The yard was enclosed on all sides by houses, which were inhabited by several poor families. Kate Reilly occupied a couple of rooms on the ground floor of one on the right-hand side. As I was preparing to make for this room, the door of which was open, I was met by a native (*Mussulman*) woman, engaged in cleaning her cooking utensils. Without getting up from the ground where she was squatting, she told me that no such person as the one I mentioned lived there. On hearing my voice, Kate called out from within in English, "Oh, yes; I'm Kate Reilly, I want to see you!" The native woman then said in Hindustanee that the "Miss Baba, had no clothes on." "I can soon put them on," called Kate from within. The woman finding herself beaten, made a last effort to prevent my seeing her mistress by running to tell her that a "sahib" (gentleman) was with me! This announcement, happily did not prevent her coming quickly. When Kate presented herself before me at the door of her room, I was horrified on seeing her. Her feet were enveloped in bandages, her legs were almost covered with sores, while an arm that was exposed to view was a mass of decay and corruption. She wore a dark petticoat reaching a little below her knees, a chemise and a red shawl thrown over one half of her shoulders, leaving the bad arm, which was too sore to be put in contact with any clothing, bare as I saw it. She is a young woman of about twenty-four years of age, of Irish parents, and has a sister a nun in a Catholic convent in Calcutta. This sister, she said, is not permitted by her religious Order to visit her, or go into the world; so she is left entirely at the mercy of the native woman, of whom I have written. Kate told me that she has well-connected relatives, but they never go near her. Her uncle pays the rent of her room, but the rest of her wants are supplied by a charitable lady, who allows her the equivalent of 30s. a month, but who is leaving for England at the end of this year, when she fears such money will no longer continue to be paid her. She was greatly troubled about this, and asked me if I thought someone would send money when her allowance was stopped. She also told me that she was very miserable in the hands of the native servant, and had tried hard, but without success, to get a native Christian woman to attend her; for if she were to die she would not like to be alone with a heathen. She said she would willingly go to the Government Leper Asylum, if suitable accommodation was provided. She had been there some years before, but was unable to stay in a room with native lepers. She asked me if things were changed now, and if she could obtain a room to herself, or one in which only white women were, if she went. I had to tell her that she could not, and, except for the fact of being entirely alone and at the mercy of her servant, she was more comfortable in her own little room. On asking if I could bring her anything, she told me she would like a mackintosh sheet, for her sores were so troublesome that she could not sleep in comfort without one. She also asked me to visit her as often as I could, and to bring others who would be her friends when I left India, as I was shortly about to do.

CHAPTER X.

ARCHDEACON MICHELL—DISPOSAL OF OUR FUND—THE LEPER CAT—THE IDIOT BOY.

As our stay in Calcutta was drawing to a close, and as I was loth to leave my leper friends without first having succeeded in interesting some influential lady or gentleman in them and their sad state, I wrote to Archdeacon Michell, and gave him a full account of my work, and asked him if he would take over my fund money, and do his best for the lepers after my departure. He sent me a kind letter in reply, promising to comply with my request, and asking me to appoint a day when he would visit with me the Leper Asylum, and also Kate Reilly. On the following Tuesday the Archdeacon and I, accompanied by Mrs.

G

Grant, my husband and Brother John, visited the lepers in the asylum, and Kate Reilly, who were all delighted on seeing so many friendly faces. Kate Reilly thanked us again and again for coming, and gave Mrs. Grant a few small commissions. She also asked for a little underclothing, and endeavoured to impress upon Archdeacon Michell her immediate want of a Christian female attendant. She told me that she had heard of a native Christian woman who was at that time living with a man, who was going away, when she could come as attendant to Kate. On remarking that this did not appear to be quite the sort of person to choose, poor Kate said that there was no such thing as choice in the matter, that only the most degraded outcasts would care to attend to lepers, and that no one would consent to take up such work if they were able to obtain a livelihood in any other way. The Reverend Mr. Michell seemed much impressed by what he had seen, and promised to go and visit Kate Reilly and the other lepers on future occasions. We arranged that he should take over what money I had left in my leper fund, and keep the books, and that Brother John would continue to visit the lepers every week as usual, taking with him anything they might require, and giving to each European and Eurasian leper a rupee, as I had been in the habit of doing. He would hand in the account of all money expended in this way, to Mr. Michell. Before leaving Calcutta I spent about £20 of the fund money in the purchase of cotton chemises, wrappers, night-gowns, and handkerchiefs for the women, and shirts for the men in the Leper Asylum; as it is necessary during the the intense heat of Calcutta to change one's underlinen frequently. When I first saw the lepers, they were complaining bitterly of the want of clean linen, and were delighted when I was able to procure a good stock of it for them. Healthy persons, even among the natives who can afford to do so, change their linen frequently during the hot weather. Those who possess no change of clothing can be seen washing their single suit, while performing their ablutions at one of the numerous tanks or bathing places in the city. If the intense heat makes bathing and a change of clothes so imperative among all persons, rich and poor, my readers will at once recognise the necessity of providing those afflicted with a loathsome evil-smelling disease like leprosy with a liberal quantity of clean linen; at least, during the hottest months of the year. I used to pity poor Daisy and Bella very much in the terrible heat. Bridget had no sores, nor did she seem affected at all like those poor girls; for there was never any bad odour discernible in her little room. I may mention that one of the peculiarities of leprosy is that those suffering from it can bear heat very badly. Hence, lepers, as a rule, like to sit in the shade and to keep out of the direct rays of the sun. I have often heard them complain that their blood seemed to be on fire. The skin of the Jewess had changed to a strange blue colour, possibly by reason of the medicines she had taken, but she was not disfigured with loathsome sores like Daisy and Bella; though she used to complain of a very unpleasant smell from her skin. Everything, even the texts on the walls in the room where Daisy was, seemed to reek of leprosy. Anyone, even with the most blunted feelings, would shudder on coming in contact with this awful smell, and could hardly fail to suggest the necessity of disinfectants for subduing it. Bridget, who was fond of animals, though I do not know how she managed to feed them, had a cat given her by Mrs. Grant. In due course, this pussy became a mother, and greatly to Bridget's delight, presented her with a fine family of tortoise-shell kittens. Mrs. Puss has, I believe, contracted leprosy; for her face is much disfigured; her eyesight has almost gone, and water was running down from her eyes, just as I have noticed in the case of certain lepers. Brother John drew my attention to this strange cat, and both of us agreed that we had never seen anything like it before. I read, some months after, that the doctors engaged on the Leprosy Commission in Simla had inoculated some rabbits with the bacillus of leprosy, and that on being killed a short time afterwards leprous tubercles or nodules had been found in their bodies. After reading that rabbits can become inoculated with leprosy, I have no doubt that Bridget's cat is afflicted with the disease, and, probably, her kittens also. In India it is not safe to stroke cats or dogs, or to allow them to sleep in beds with children; for it is possible for them to transmit disease from place to place. Sorry as I would be to deprive poor Bridget of any small pleasure, I must say that I do not think a cat should be kept in a leper Asylum; for it is almost impossible to keep one shut up or control her movements at all times, and there is nothing to prevent her, after having been stroked by lepers, and licking their sores, from going to a healthy person and being kissed and fondled by young children.

I drew the attention of the public, through the medium of our paper, to a native idiot boy, who, though not a leper, had been an inmate of the Calcutta Leper Asylum for a long time. It appears, from what Mr. McGuire told me, that some years ago, a native child who was deformed in such a manner as to render walking or standing impossible, and who used to move along the ground in a sitting position, was found outside the leper Asylum. The lepers had fed him and he, although not a leper, had been allowed to live with them in the Asylum. When I remarked on the danger of allowing him to live entirely with lepers, and to eat and sleep with them, and suggested his removal, Mr. McGuire informed me that there was no place where he, a deformed harmless lunatic, could be put, and that he had lived with the lepers for many years, being doubtless perfectly happy. This boy is in the Calcutta Leper Asylum at the time of writing, and, so far, has not developed any indications of having contracted the disease. Another native, a very bad leper, was turned out of the Asylum into the streets for misbehaviour. Here we have a leper covered with sores expelled from the Asylum by Mr. McGuire, and with, I presume, full sanction of the Commissioner of police, for refusing to maintain order within its walls. In the Bombay Asylum there are cells for refractory subjects; but in Calcutta they are sent out with their disease and misery into the streets to mix with healthy persons, and to prove a source of danger to all those with whom they come in contact. They are not again entitled to even the wretched shelter and protection afforded at the Calcutta Leper Asylum. It is high time that such scandals as these were made known, and that prompt action be taken by Government for the segregation of very bad lepers like the man of whom I speak; for when he called on me at my house to tell his story, his running sores were without bandages, and my little boy was playing quite close to where he was squatting. Besides, in the crowded Bazaars of Calcutta, he would come into close contact with a number of healthy native children, who go about quite naked, and who might become inoculated with this disease.

CHAPTER XI.

THE NUNS OF LORETTO CONVENT.

I AM very glad to say that I received much kind sympathy and help in my work from the Nuns of the Loretto Convent. Although a member of the Church of England, I found the Reverend Mother Provincial, Mother Mechtilda, Mother Antonia, and the sisters at Loretto House, took the deepest interest in my labours among the lepers, and used, by their kindly advice and monetary assistance, to encourage and aid me in every possible way. I first became acquainted with them through sending my little boy to school at their convent in the hills. During the hot weather, it is found necessary to send as many children as their parents can afford to pay for, away out of the heat of

Calcutta, to the cooler climate of Darjeeling or any adjacent hill station, where the little ones remain till the temperature becomes sufficiently cool for them to return to their studies in the plains. I sent my boy one season to Darjeeling with the nuns, and it was when arranging for his trip that I first met my kind friends. I used to like going to them; for all was very peaceful at Lorretto. It was no uncommon sight to see a beggar seated at the convent gate eating a meal that the nuns had brought him; it being their custom never to send a hungry person away without giving him any food there might be in the convent. Poor persons, knowing this, used often to get a meal from the nuns. When I rang the bell I was always certain of a warm-hearted reception; for one or more of my friends were sure to be at home, and, being all Irishwomen, my welcome was cordial and sincere. Their pretty drawing-room was in no way richly or grandly furnished; but comfort rather than effect was studied within the convent.

The glare of the sun was shut out, fresh flowers were always on the table; while the gold and silver fish swimming about in a bowl looked cool and refreshing. A number of religious engravings and a quantity of exquisite crewel work, which was done by the pupils and nuns, gave the room a more homely look than one usually finds in drawing-rooms abroad.

The nuns themselves, in their clean white gowns, devoid of drapery or any ornamentation, are so kind and womanly that one's heart goes out to them at once. Before I had known the dear old Mother Provincial an hour, I found myself telling her of all my woes and troubles, and, encouraged by her kindness, I felt better able, after such visits, to do battle with the world; for there is nothing so comforting as the genuine sympathy of one woman with another. She would give me an encouraging tap on the shoulder, and say, "Go on, dear; continue to do your best for those poor lepers, and we will pray for you; all the nuns will pray for the success of such a work as yours. It is so nice to see the young thoughtfully working for the sorely afflicted." Mother Provincial not only encouraged me with words, but she got up a subscription among the nuns and sent me a sum of money for my leper fund. She did all this in her quiet, sweet way, knowing that I professed a different creed to that of her own ; but she waived all prejudice, because she thought I was doing a good work. I have nothing but the pleasantest and most grateful recollections of the nuns ; for I invariably found them the same kind friends, through good and evil report, all the time I was in Calcutta. They must have heard and read enough deprecatory remarks about me to have turned them entirely against me, had not they thoroughly believed in my sincerity ; for interested persons, who did not believe that anyone would work in an honest cause when actuated only by motives of justice— we won't say charity—wrote their views about me in the local papers, in which they tried to hold me up to derision. However, the public, knowing that I personally had nothing to gain, and that I could find no possible pleasure in going into the haunts of disease, other than that of aiding those who could in no way help themselves, gave me their support, and money was sent me from time to time to spend on comforts for the lepers. I think I have to thank the nuns for a great deal of the money that came to me ; for these ladies possess unbounded influence among a large number of right-thinking persons, and they used it on behalf of the lepers, so that many rupees were sent to me through them.

One day I caused no little surprise and amusement by asking Mother Mechtilda to come and take afternoon tea with me. It was from her I learnt that they never leave the convent except to go to another, nor do they walk in the public streets. I ventured to say that it was a pity such good women should shut themselves up when they might be doing work in the world among the poor and sick. "We are not," they replied, "permitted by our Order to go out; we teach the young. There are nuns, sisters of charity, the Little Sisters of the Poor, and many other Orders, whose work takes them into the world. We teach and help to clothe poor children."

While telling me this, a bell rang, and the Mother, asking me to excuse her, knelt down in the room where we were sitting, and prayed for a few minutes, after which we resumed our conversation. I should have liked to have asked her what bell it was that summoned her to prayer, but did not like to discuss such a solemn subject as this would be to her. They never sent me away without a nice bouquet of fresh flowers, which would be picked from the garden while I waited. This pretty token was generally accompanied by a hearty "God bless you" as I turned to leave the convent. They were not so exclusively devoted to serious subjects as to forget the bodily wants of their visitors. On hot days a refreshing glass of iced lemonade and biscuits were always ready, and one's requirements often anticipated with kindly forethought before they were made known. I am sorry to say that I was hurried away from Calcutta by telegram before I could pay a farewell visit to my kind friends. I feel sure I have no more sincere well-wishers in this work than the nuns of Loretto Convent, the memory of whose kind words and actions shall always be gratefully treasured up in my heart.

CHAPTER XII.

MEDICINE—NO WARM BATHS—AN UGLY LOOKING-GLASS—
CHRISTMAS DAY IN THE LEPER ASYLUM—THE LEPER
BOY—MR. BAILEY.

AT the Leper Asylum things were not looking bright. Dr. Unna's medicine, which had arrived from London, had not been getting a fair trial. The European doctor under whose supervision it was given, having himself no faith in any of the prescribed cures for leprosy, had not placed his patients under a regular course of treatment. He was a doctor in practice in Calcutta, and we cannot blame him for refusing to personally superintend the treatment of lepers. A practitioner who was known to go regularly among lepers would find people chary of consulting him about ordinary ailments, and his practice would suffer in consequence. The lepers had the medicine; he would give instructions as to its application; but whether they took it or not was their own affair. An inmate of the Almshouse, who had been an apothecary, was employed in giving out the drugs used by the lepers, but there was no skilled doctor to superintend or be present when these medicines were administered. Daisy refused to try Dr. Unna's medicine. When I asked her reason for doing so, after being so anxious for it to arrive, she told me that she would agree to take the pills, but that a greasy kind of ointment had to be rubbed over the body, and that, as there was no warm water procurable in which she could bathe, she would wait till the hot months, when she could take a bath and wash off the grease. This, I may explain, happened during what is known as the cold weather, when the lepers found it impossible to take cold baths; so preferred, in the absence of any warm ones, to do without. The attendant who was paid from our fund should have been told, if there had been any supervision over her, to provide warm baths for her charges; but being a low-class native woman, who preferred to do as little work as possible for her salary, she, of course, did not care to burden herself with the extra trouble of procuring warm water, when not compelled to do so. Besides, it was altogether without precedent that any "medical comfort," such as a warm bath, should be allowed to any inmate of the Calcutta Leper Asylum. The Jewess, who had been using the medicine, had, she said, derived much benefit from it. I should have liked to have consulted some of the officials about this medicine, as Kate Reilly had asked for some of it to try; but, although nearly a year had elapsed since I first began my visits to the lepers, these gentlemen chose to maintain their hostile attitude towards me. I asked Mr. McGuire whether any of the ointment could be procured for the use of lepers who were living outside of the Asylum, and he said it could not, so I was not able to give any to Kate Reilly. Bridget troubled herself little about the new medicine; for, happily, there were no sores on her body, none of her fingers or toes were distorted, and she did not appear to be suffering from the lassitude that seemed to so much depress the spirits of the other inmates. She was always ready to burden me with orders for the most ridiculous things, all of which she would have me write down on my tablets in her presence. On one occasion she wanted a doll's house, and was very angry with me because I failed to find and take one of the kind she fancied. Another day she asked for a looking-glass, as she hadn't seen her face, she said, for twenty years! I took her a little ornamental thing; but when she looked into it and saw her face, she got very angry and said she had never seen such an ugly looking-glass in her life! I peered into it, and said that it seemed to be all right, "Yes" she replied with her rich Irish brogue, "Its all very well for the young, no matter how ugly they are, youth is always beautiful. Its the old people, like me, who want nice looking-glasses." Brother John smiled at the one-sided compliment I had received, and we agreed to take her another glass that would not "make her look ugly." As we left the asylum, we heard Bridget's voice calling "Now, Mr. Jack (Brother John), don't forget to remember the looking-glass!" Bridget had got into a childish way of wanting everything she saw; so when we used to visit her with things for the other inmates in the basket, she would always pry into it and say, "What's that?" "Whose going to get that?"

"Why don't you bring me this?" and so on, till we were obliged to adopt the plan of going to her room after we had been the round of the other wards, and when the basket was denuded of all the things but those that we had brought for her. One day when I told her I was going to leave India, she sent Brother John out of the room, and said in her most coaxing manner, " Give me a good character to the new people who come when you go, or they won't bring me anything. Don't tell them that I ask for things belonging to the others; I say, give me a good character to them!" Poor old Bridget had led such a hard life that I suppose it had become natural to her to think of herself before anyone. She was very peculiar at times, and her mind used to wander. She would then talk in a strange manner about her young days. From what she used to say on those occasions, I learned that she had been a corset maker, and used to sit " stitching away night and day, stitching away." Sometimes she would repeat these words over and over again, and appear entirely oblivious of our presence; then, after talking disjointedly for a few minutes, she would gaze on some flowers I had brought, and say suddenly:

"Faded old roses, why don't you bring me fresh flowers?" I would endeavour to explain that the long drive in the heat from my house down to the asylum had made them droop, and tell her, that if she put them in water they would revive. But while I was speaking she would be "havering" about something else, and not hearing a word of what I was saying. Sometimes, if she thought we stayed longer with Daisy or any of the others than with her, she would get angry and say some very uncomplimentary things about us all; but we used to take it in good part, for poor old Bridget was not quite right in her head. At times she used to almost frighten me with the weird stories of ghosts and devils whom she said she saw walking about the place. She would call me to her and say, "This place is full of devils; there are devils everywhere, and dead bones all under this room. You don't know what goes on here at night, and they are all devils; I scream and scream and no one comes, because the place is all full of devils." We used to tell her that it was all imagination; but she was never tired of talking to us about their depredations. She was a confirmed miser, and used to put away all the different articles of clothing I would bring her from time to time, instead of wearing them. She said she wanted them "to keep." It amused her to have a gay apron or dressing-gown and fold it and put it in a box, in order that she might take it out and admire it, when she wanted something pretty to look at.

My readers will have doubtless discovered for themselves that, among the female lepers, the one I liked best of all was Daisy. Bella was a dear girl too, but seldom spoke to anyone. The Jewess was kind and nice; but, like Bridget, would show great disappointment if I happened to forget anything she had asked for. Daisy was always the same. Whatever I took to her she received with grateful thanks; but, above all, she liked my regular visits to her. She had a good heart, and was full of gentle, affectionate regard for Bella, whom she used to treat like a younger sister. Everything that Daisy said or did was right in Bella's eyes. The two were inseparable. Daisy, who used to generally superintend Bridget's *ménage* as far as she was able, used often to tell me of the old woman's vagaries, many of which caused general amusement. The Jewess, who spoke with a strong German accent, would at times mispronounce words in a way that would make Daisy laugh. On seeing this, she would get very angry and sulk for a long time. I may mention that some foreigners, like ourselves, have a great dislike to be laughed at, and often treat what is in reality a harmless joke as a serious insult. However, Daisy could not refrain from laughing merrily at times over some of the peculiar mistakes of the Jewess, thereby making that lady so seriously angry that a lengthened coolness between them would be the result. The Jewess would tell me about these squabbles, and ask me to speak seriously to Daisy; but, when I did so, Daisy said that without wishing to give offence or hurt the other's feelings in any way, she found it impossible to refrain from laughing when the Jewess said such funny things as she often did. As Christmas was fast approaching, Daisy, seconded of course by Bella, asked me to go and see them on Christmas day. She tried to speak calmly about my departure from India, but broke down and burst into tears. Instead of comforting her, I cried too, and felt very sorry and miserable. On Christmas morning I took with me as many gay and cheery reminders of the season in the way of bonbons and "goodies" as I could think of. The male ward had been all decorated by the little leper boy with coloured written inscriptions. "Glory to God in the Highest" was arranged over the entrance to their cheerless abode, and near it, on a square of pink paper, the words, "God bless Captain Hayes, God bless Mrs. Hayes and Brother John." This remained up on the entrance to the ward for a long time, till all the decorations were taken down. Daisy and the others had not decorated their ward, but they wished us all a "Merry Christmas," and thanked us again and again for coming on that day into such a sorrowful abode as the Leper Asylum. I found it hard to be cheerful and wish them a "Merry Christmas" in return. It seemed such a mockery to suggest mirth to them. The gay crackers, with their tinsel and bright colours, looked out of place there. Christmas, with its joy and gladness, seemed to bring no comfort to their sad hearts. I admired the decorations in the male ward, and accepted a bouquet of roses from my young leper friend, whose face beamed with pleasure as he handed them to me. The flowers had been most carefully arranged by the child, who is a real artist, with a keen eye for the beautiful, and I felt sorry as I threw away his offering afterwards, when out of sight of the Leper Hospital; for I could not take home anything from that infected place. Daisy had commissioned Mrs. Smith, the matron of the Almshouse, to purchase for me a small workbox, while Bella ordered a blotting-pad, both of which Mrs. Smith was to get and present to me in their presence on Christmas morning. I never remember in my life receiving any presents that I was so pleased to get. Mrs. Smith, Daisy, Bella and myself were all in tears during their presentation, so there was no speech-making or eloquence displayed. I could not even utter a word of thanks, but stood like a fool crying silently, and trying to hide my tears by busying myself in taking the things I had brought out of the basket. Brother John, who had been a spectator of the scene, was shedding tears, too, I think; for he had turned his face away, and was using his handkerchief as if he had suddenly contracted a bad cold in his head. I cannot in any way describe this scene in all its sadness. Poor Bella and Daisy were such very bad lepers that they could not have handed the presents to me, even if they had tried, and it seemed inexpressibly kind of them to get for me their thoughtfully-selected and useful gifts. I tried to say a few cheerful things about Christmas, and to interest them in the gay crackers, cards, and various things I took out of the basket; but my words seemed to fall flat, and a great sadness settled on all of us. Daisy and Bella were sitting together in silence while I deposited my things on their little table; so, as I could think of nothing cheerful to say, nor was able to trust myself to speak it, even if I had, I dried my eyes and went to Bridget's room. She had a great deal to tell me, and rattled along in joyful glee at seeing all the pretty crackers and cards and the bright colours that she loved so well. The Jewess, too, was very pleased with what we took her, and "wondered who would be so kind to her when I had gone." I found the men sad and depressed. Ramey, who was not feeling so well as usual, seemed to be much troubled in his mind about my departure, and began speculating where we should all be by next Christmas. He had a favour to ask: it was that I would give him a photograph of myself and husband before leaving, and thanked me very much for my kindness to him.

Then tears filled his eyes and he broke down utterly. Little Underwood, the boy who gave me the flowers, on seeing Ramey, began to cry too, so instead of having a "merry" Christmas, ours was an extremely sad one. When I went a short time after that to the asylum to bid them good-bye, I had made up my mind to say all sorts of nice things to them; but none of them were really uttered, for we all cried again. Daisy said, "We won't say good-bye, but——" whatever she was going to say was not said; for she cried and could not go on. I told them that Brother John would continue to visit them as usual. "Yes," said Ramey, "but you have fought so bravely for us." They were all glad, however, to receive the news of Brother John's intended visits, and I promised that they should hear from me from time to time. I also told them that Archdeacon Michell had consented to interest himself in their welfare. Next day, as I was driving out of my gate, I was surprised to see little Underwood, who had walked all the way from the Leper Asylum to bid me good-bye! He blushed and looked in a most sheepish manner at some drooping flowers he held in his hand, as if ashamed to offer them to me. I could see he was pleased when I accepted them and thanked him. The gratitude of these poor lepers to me for the little I had been able to do for them was very real and honest, and will always remain in my mind as a solemn and holy memory.

The doctors engaged on the Leprosy Commission have visited the inmates of the Calcutta Asylum, have had them photographed, and made a number of inquiries into the antecedents of each leper; but up to the present nothing has been done by Government for the proper housing or immediate relief of these sufferers. What I have written has been done in the earnest hope that their cause will be taken up by some kind people, who will act promptly in establishing them where they will receive the kindness and care accorded to sick people.

Mr. McGuire, the superintendent, is a stern disciplinarian and an admirable man to deal with the number of loafers and bad characters who infest the streets of Calcutta; but he is not equally well suited to administer to the requirements of fragile leper women, who need kind and gentle treatment under their load of affliction. Mrs. Smith, the matron of the almshouse, is a subordinate to Mr. McGuire, and possesses little or no power in her position. I found her a good-hearted woman, who tried in many ways to be kind to the lepers; but, as she unfortunately does not have the handling of any money, she cannot order the requisite changes of underlinen for them or administer to their wants as a woman in authority would be able to do. Mr. McGuire has to be applied to for everything they require, an arrangement which, to be satisfactory, I need hardly say should always be entrusted to a woman.

I was able to obtain a small sum of money from a charitable lady for Kate Reilly, and handed it over to Archdeacon Michell, with the request that it might be spent in providing her with anything she may require, rather than to give it over to the care of the native servant to dispose of as she thinks fit. Brother John has promised to visit her often, and Mrs. Grant will also go as frequently as she can to her, as well as to the Leper Asylum. The other leper pensioners will receive their money from Archdeacon Michell as usual, and I shall try my utmost to keep up the fund; for it is a source of much comfort to these poor lepers to be provided with little things that they are otherwise unable to obtain.

I was interested in reading a short account of the Calcutta Leper Asylum, in a book called " A Glimpse at the Indian Mission Fields and Leper Asylums," written by Mr. Wellesley Bailey, a Scotch missionary, who visited the Calcutta Leper Asylum in 1886, in which, speaking of January 19th, he says :—" Before breakfast spent an hour and a-half in the Leper Asylum and had a very interesting interview with Miss J—— [Daisy]. I read and prayed with her, and she seemed very grateful for the visit, poor thing. I took some books with me, which had been given me by a friend in the north of Scotland, and gave them away to those who could speak English. I only wish my friend could have seen the delight which her gifts produced on that dismal abode, and it would have gladdened her own heart." Later on we read :— " January 21st. After breakfast drove over (a long distance) to Belvidere to see the Lieutenant-Governor, Sir Rivers Thompson, who was kind enough to spare me a few minutes of his very valuable time. His Honour received me most kindly, and listened attentively to what I had to say. My object in calling was to explain to him the over-crowded state of the Leper Asylum, and to ask him if he would use his influence to get something done before his term of office expired, which it is about to do immediately. He said that the only way the thing could be done was to get the District Charitable Society to move in the matter; and that if they make an application to him he would see what could be done. But the time was short and the formalities which would have to be gone through were long, and so nothing could be done." With these words Mr. Bailey dismisses the Calcutta Leper Asylum from his book, and proceeds to describe his visit to Darjeeling. He does not mention Bridget, Bella, or the Jewess; probably he was unable to visit all the English-speaking lepers, or he would have done so. Anderson and Phillipe, an Englishman and a Frenchman, are lepers who have recently been admitted into the male ward, so Mr. Bailey could not have met them in 1886.

To use the words of a friend, I may say that the thought of "a good time is coming" for those who suffer in this life is, no doubt, full of comfort to the afflicted ones themselves; but surely this same thought is largely responsible for our indifference to the sufferings of others. So long as the slaves of self are sure that God will "make it up in the end," so long will their selfishness be justified by their belief. Thus the righteousness of God becomes an excuse for the uncharity of men.

CHAPTER XIII.

LEPERS IN BOMBAY—A LECTURE AT THE SOROSIS
CLUB—OUR DEPARTURE FROM INDIA.

IN passing through Bombay, just before our departure from India, I called on Mr. Ackworth, the Municipal Commissioner, who has the interests of lepers at heart, and who by dint of much earnest endeavour succeeded in raising Rs. 75,000 for the erection of a Leper Home at Matoonga, near Bombay. In this institution, which is admirably conducted in every way, I saw 210 native male and female lepers. There were no Europeans. Mr. Ackworth informed me that if European lepers presented themselves for admittance at the Home, separate buildings would be erected for them, and their comfort studied as far as possible. I found all the wards well ventilated, and, although there were 210 lepers in the buildings, no unpleasant odours were discernible above the smell of the disinfectants employed. The native women lepers have two female nurses to attend on them, and there is also a competent staff of men to dress and assist the inmates of the male ward. A regular staff of doctors, under the supervision of Doctor Weir, attend the lepers, and a resident surgeon is always on the spot. The Matoonga Asylum is about five miles out of Bombay, and is hidden from the high road by trees and foliage. Mr. Ackworth is having flowers planted in the gardens, with a view of interesting his patients in gardening as a pastime. The lepers in this institution are not allowed to return to their old occupation of begging in the streets. They are told, on entering, that they will never be allowed to go out. Mr. Ackworth possesses no legal power of detention over these lepers, but in order to make them believe otherwise, has discovered an old municipal law which is sufficiently elastic to enable him to use it in clearing the streets and crowded slums of Bombay of lepers and persons suffering from an infectious or contagious disease.

On the occasion of my visit, Dr. Weir and Dr. Charles accompanied Mr. Ackworth and myself, and we made the tour of inspection together. I noticed several Catholic rosaries hanging up near the beds of the lepers and found, on inquiry, that these sufferers were regularly visited by their priest. I asked Mr. Ackworth if any of our Protestant clergymen had visited the lepers, and he told me that although one had clamoured to have his name put on the Committee of the Institution, and had got this done; he had never visited its inmates or seemed to trouble himself any further about them! While we were talking, a native leper was led out of one of the male wards by an attendant. He sunk down near the building in a state of great exhaustion, and called out, in his own language, some words which Dr. Weir told me were to the effect that he was dying, and that he begged us to save him. Poor man! he knew that these gentlemen had been kind to him in giving him a home, in binding up his sores, and in relieving his sufferings by all that medical skill could accomplish; so I suppose he thought that men so mighty as these *sahibs* were; could stay the hand of death, if they so willed. He had accordingly persuaded one of the ward boys to lead him into the presence of his benefactors in order that they might see his misery. He was lifted with difficulty back again into the ward and placed on his bed; for he had craved what no mortal man could possibly give him—life. The rays of the setting sun fell on his face, which showed a piteous expression of misery and despair. I turned away and gazed around at the glorious light of the sun on the sea in the distance—a beautiful blue sea on which numbers of boats with their white sails unfurled were gliding peacefully to and fro—and then on the white tombstones by the hillside denoting the resting place of a few strugglers who have gone before; when Mr. Ackworth reminded me that the shadows were lengthening, and that we should have to start on our drive back. After inspecting the kitchen, surgery and store-rooms, all of which are models in their way, we waved adieu to the many lepers who had congregated to give us their parting *salaams* and drove away to Bombay. I thought of poor Daisy, Bridget, Bella, the Jewess, and of the male lepers huddled together in that pestilent Calcutta Asylum, and wished I could have transferred them to the kindly charge of Mr. Ackworth and Dr. Weir. As we drove along, Dr. Charles told me that he was about to sail for London on the following day, adding that we ought to try and help Mr. Ackworth in obtaining funds for carrying on his institution. Government allows Rs.1,000, I think, monthly towards defraying expenses, but Mr. Ackworth wished to enlarge the buildings, as many more lepers were asking for admittance, and funds are needed. Dr. Charles entered heartily into my scheme of providing comforts for the European and Eurasian lepers, and gave it as his opinion that our own people are terribly neglected in India, where almost everything that is done by public charity is for the sole and exclusive benefit of Natives. He promised to do his utmost to help me and my cause if he met me in England, as he considered that it was the duty of every Englishman and woman to assist the sick and suffering of their own country wherever and whenever they could do so.

In Bombay there is a club exclusively for ladies called the "Sorosis," which is presided over by Dr. E. B. Ryder, an American lady with a kind heart, a clear head, and a great love for all the members of her own sex. She received me most kindly when I called on her. She seemed so interested in my work among the Calcutta lepers, that I sent her a portion of this book in manuscript to read. On the following day she called to ask me if I would go to the Sorosis Club and tell the ladies, about twenty in number, who would be assembled there to meet me, of my work among the lepers. I had a most attentive and sympathetic audience of kind-hearted ladies on this occasion, all of whom shed tears when I told them of the grateful kindness of the poor lepers to me, and of their sad and lonely life. One lady took the address of Archdeacon Michell, and promised to try and send some money for my friends, and so keep in touch with them. Dr. Ryder said that if I were to lecture in England on their behalf, I would get money; and that I carried my audience with my earnestness in telling my story. I need hardly say that I would be only too happy to take her hint, if I could work it out effectively.

Dr. Ryder and the kind-hearted ladies of the Sorosis Club, in wishing me good-bye, expressed a desire that copies of this book should be sent to them as soon as it was published, and heartily wished me " God speed " in my work. It was very soothing to my feelings to receive kindness and offers of help in work for which I had suffered so many rebuffs. When I embarked on board the ss. *Calabria*, which was to take us home, I felt that with their kind words in my ears I could sit down and work at my book with renewed vigour, feeling sure that women as kind and sympathetic as my Bombay friends, would read it with interest in England, and that perhaps something might be done for my poor leper friends in Calcutta. When we reached Aden I posted a long letter to Daisy, telling her of what I was doing, and promising to send them something from London. I asked her to cause my letter to be read to Ramey, and the other male lepers, and promised to keep her posted up from time to time in anything that might be of interest to them.

Just as this book is going to press, I have received a letter from Mrs. Grant, who tells me that all the European and Eurasian inmates of the Calcutta Leper Asylum are much in the same way as when I left them, except Ramey, who is very ill, and is not expected to live long. I deeply regret to hear that Mrs. Smith died suddenly of heart disease. The poor lepers lost a kind friend in her. Mrs. Grant is working bravely in this good cause, and has stimulated interest in these helpless sufferers.

CHAPTER XIV.

REMARKS ON LEPROSY.

By Surgeon-Major G. G. MacLaren, M.D.

LEPROSY, as is well known, is a disease prevalent all over the world, from Norway and Sweden in the north, to India and China in the east, and to Australia and the Islands of the Southern Seas.

My own personal experience, however, has been limited only to India, where I have had the disease under close observation for nearly twenty years. It would be out of place to enter into any technical or scientific description of its nature and progress in a work of this kind. All are aware that a Commission, composed of five men, most competent to undertake the investigation of the history of the disease in all its bearings, is now sitting in India, and their report, which will be made public at the end of the year, will doubtless give information which will be of the utmost value in establishing means for its amelioration and, probably, ultimate extinction. My service in India has placed me in a district where, unfortunately, leprosy is exceedingly prevalent amongst the native population, although not entirely limited to those alone; for I have had cases of Europeans also to deal with. This led me to take the matter up, more from the hope of relieving suffering than from any other motive, the miserable victims being allowed to wander about as simple beggars, outcasts from their own friends and villages. They thus transform themselves, if not into a danger to their fellow-creatures, at least into a most objectionable nuisance and eye-sore to the whole community. To look upon the streets and roads of an Indian Station on Sunday morning (and this was the manner these wretched creatures adopted to enlist the sympathies of their fellow beings in my own station), lined with rows of lepers, exhibiting their disgusting sores and their maimed and deformed bodies to the public gaze, was a sight that could not fail to touch the hardest and most indifferent heart. To prevent the daily exhibition of these harrowing scenes, I enlisted the sympathy of the general public, and was able, as shown in the report of the Dehra Dun Leper Asylum, mentioned elsewhere in this work, to establish and endow a retreat for all who would take advantage of its comforts and benefits. I had no difficulty whatever in inducing all the afflicted—old and young, men and women—to take up their quarters therein. Before admission, all agree to become *permanent* residents and to live apart. I had studied with care the beneficial effects of segregation which had been adopted in the retreats in Norway and Sweden, with the marked diminution in the number of cases imported during the decades succeeding the foundation of these institutions, and, acting on this principle, the Dehra Dun Leper Asylum was opened in 1879, and has been in existence ever since. There the sexes are strictly segregated, and the inmates live and are cared for under the most happy conditions. Throughout those years I have had constant opportunity, there, of studying the nature and progress of the disease.

Being a firm believer in the hereditary transmission of all ailments—or the tendency to them, both mental and physical—I have traced *direct* transmission in at

MALE LEPERS. [p. 123.

least thirty per cent. of the cases coming under my observation. The disease is doubtless due, like most others, to the presence of a *bacillus* in the blood, and if there be not direct transmission of this from parent to child, its effects are undoubtedly hereditary. These, however, are points which I need not discuss, for they will be specially considered by the Leprosy Commissioners. Acting on the strength of my own convictions as to the transmissibility and communicability of leprosy, I established the Dehra Dun Asylum on the principle already noted, and it has answered so far admirably; all its inmates living as happily as they can, under their unfortunate conditions, and ending their existence contentedly! I have had, of course, ample opportunity of studying the nature of the disease, and its effects on the different organs of the body, and in the many examinations I have made, *post mortem*, I can testify that not a single organ in the whole body is exempt from the attacks and inroads of this dire and loathsome malady. It invades the brain, spinal nerves, the eyes, tongue and throat, the lungs, the liver, and other digestive organs. In addition, as is generally known, it maims and deforms the external parts of the body in a manner too revolting to describe. It is painful to witness the amount of deplorable suffering some of these creatures endure. True it is that many feel but little pain—one of the forms of the disease producing *anæsthesia*, or insensibility of the parts affected; but this is the case in a few only. The majority suffer in variously painful degrees, according to the organ or part implicated, and it is a mistake to think that their sufferings are little. Many, in the earlier forms of the ailment, lose their sense of sight, smell and taste, and when their lungs or throat is attacked (a common form), their agonies are dreadfully distressing and painful to behold. The inroads of the disease are slow and gradual, which makes it all the more trying, and the painful and lingering death to which most are doomed is a condition that one dreads to dwell on.

Added to all this there is a peculiarly penetrating odour common to lepers, whether they be Europeans or natives of India, constantly emanating from their bodies, which makes contact, or even close conversation, with those afflicted, most objectionable. During my medical experience of over

25 years, I have had, of course, to deal with all sorts of ailments; but the odour evolved from the leper's body is one so peculiar and " sickening " that I fail to find words to exactly describe it. The effects of a visit to a leper asylum, or to a single individual leper with whom I have had to remain in conversation, produces a sensation quite dissimilar to that resulting from personal contact with any other disease. A peculiar sensation is produced in the mouth, and an irresistible feeling that one has inhaled some disgusting and noxious material, which clings to the tongue, the lining membrane of the mouth and fauces. This feeling lasts for sometimes fifteen minutes after my visit has ended, and is not entirely removed until I have overcome it by smoking a pipe or cigar. This result is (it certainly is not fancy) one that should be strongly impressed on the general public, and be accepted as a powerful argument in favour of secluding all lepers from contact, either directly or indirectly, with any body or thing that is likely to prove a means of communicability. It may not be out of place here to mention that since 1875 I have given the most careful attention to the treatment of leprosy, tried

most conscientiously all the various drugs that have been from time to time recommended, and used unsparingly and for prolonged periods all outward applications that have been brought to notice, and must frankly admit that I have not witnessed the least *permanent* benefit from any one of these. There are different forms of the disease described in books, but my experience has been that these are simply external or special manifestations, all resulting from the same single cause, determined for the special locality in the system of the particular organ attacked. *Once a leper, always a leper*, is the sad outcome of my many years close observation, let the treatment be what it may. It behoves us, therefore, as human beings, simply to do all in our power, in whatever part of the world leprosy prevails, to establish retreats in which its victims can be housed in seclusion, apart from intercourse with the general public, where they can obtain proper shelter, be provided with suitable food and clothing, and where medical comforts can be placed at their disposal. All such institutions should be built and conducted on the best sanitary hygienic principles; each being suited to its own special locality and class of inmates. By these means assuredly will the disease cease to extend, and thus, in all probability, ultimately be exterminated. This happy result had been accomplished in instances of other allied diseases, simply from the adoption of improved sanitary surroundings, and it is not too far to look forward to a like result in the case of even such a loathsome, repulsive, and vile a malady as leprosy.

No. 47. September, 1891.

A Catalogue of Finely Illustrated Works, published by THACKER, SPINK & CO., Calcutta To be obtained also of THACKER & CO., Limited, Bombay, and W. THACKER & CO., 87 Newgate Street, London.

THACKER, SPINK & CO., CALCUTTA.

Third Edition, Imperial 16mo. Rs. 4-8. (6s.)

BEHIND THE BUNGALOW.
BY EHA,
AUTHOR OF "TRIBES ON MY FRONTIER."

WITH FIFTY-THREE CLEVER SKETCHES
By the Illustrator of "The Tribes."

As "The Tribes on my Frontier" graphically and humorously described the Animal Surroundings of an Indian Bungalow, the present work describes with much pleasantry the Human Officials thereof, with their peculiarities, idiosyncrasies, and, to the European, strange methods of duty. Each chapter contains Character Sketches by the Illustrator of "The Tribes," and the work is a "Natural History" of the Native Tribes who in India render us service.

W. THACKER & CO., LONDON.

"There is plenty of fun in 'Behind the Bungalow,' and more than fun for those with eyes to see. These sketches may have an educational purpose beyond that of mere amusement; they show through all their fun a keen observation of native character and a just appreciation of it."
—*The World.*

BEHIND THE BUNGALOW.
By the Author of "*TRIBES ON MY FRONTIER.*"
AND ILLUSTRATED BY THE SAME ARTIST.

"'The Tribes On My Frontier' was very good : 'Behind the Bungalow' is even better. Anglo-Indians will see how truthful are these sketches. People who know nothing about India will delight in the clever drawings and the truly humorous descriptions; and, their appetite for fun being gratified, they will not fail to note the undercurrent of sympathy."
—*The Graphic.*

"The native members of an Anglo-Indian household are hit off with great fidelity and humour."—*The Queen.*

THACKER, SPINK & CO., CALCUTTA.

Fourth Edition. In Imperial 16mo, uniform with "Lays of Ind," "Riding," "Hindu Mythology," etc. *Rs.* 6. (8*s.* 6*d.*)

THE TRIBES ON MY FRONTIER:

An Indian Naturalist's Foreign Policy.

By EHA.

WITH FIFTY ILLUSTRATIONS BY F. C. MACRAE.

N this remarkably clever work there are most graphically and humorously described the surroundings of a Mofussil bungalow. The twenty chapters embrace a year's experiences, and provide endless sources of amusement and suggestion. The numerous able illustrations add very greatly to the interest of the volume, which will find a place on every table.

THE CHAPTERS ARE—

I.—A Durbar.
II.—The Rats.
III.—The Mosquitos.
IV.—The Lizards.
V.—The Ants.
VI.—The Crows.
VII.—The Bats.
VIII.—Bees, Wasps, et hoc genus omne.
IX.—The Spiders.
X.—The Butterfly : Hunting Him.
XI.—The Butterfly : Contemplating Him.
XII.—The Frogs.
XIII.—The Bugs.
XIV.—The Birds of the Garden.
XV.—The Birds at the Mango Tope.
XVI.—The Birds at the Tank.
XVII.—The Poultry Yard.
XVIII.—The White Ants.
XIX.—The Hypodermatikosyringophoroi.
XX.—Etcetera.

W. THACKER & CO., LONDON.

THE TRIBES ON MY FRONTIER.
Fourth Edition. Rs. 6. (8s 6d.)

"It is a very clever record of a year's observations round the bungalow in 'Dustypore.' . . . . It is by no means a mere travesty. . . . . The writer is always amusing, and never dull."—*Field*.

"The book is cleverly illustrated by Mr. F. C. Macrae. We have only to thank our Anglo-Indian naturalist for the delightful book which he has sent home to his countrymen in Britain. May he live to give us another such."—*Chambers' Journal*.

"A most charming series of sprightly and entertaining essays on what may be termed the fauna of the Indian bungalow. . . , . We have no doubt that this amusing book will find its way into every Anglo-Indian's library."—*Allen's Indian Mail*.

"This is a delightful book, irresistibly funny in description and illustration, but full of genuine science too. . . . . . There is not a dull or uninstructive page in the whole book."—*Knowledge*.

"It is a pleasantly-written book about the insects and other torments of India which make Anglo-Indian life unpleasant, and which can be read with pleasure even by those beyond the reach of the tormenting things Eha describes."—*Graphic*.

"The volume is full of accurate and unfamiliar observation."
—*Saturday Review*.

THACKER, SPINK & CO., CALCUTTA.

In Imperial 16mo. Uniform with "Lays of Ind," "Hindu Mythology," etc.
Handsomely bound. Rs. 7-8. (10s. 6d.)

RIDING FOR LADIES.
With Hints on the Stable.
BY MRS. POWER O'DONOGHUE.
AUTHOR OF "LADIES ON HORSEBACK," "A BEGGAR ON HORSEBACK," etc.

With 91 Illustrations drawn expressly for the Work by A. Chantrey Corbould.

HIS able and beautiful volume will form a Standard on the Subject, and is one which no lady can dispense with. The scope of the work will be understood by the following:

CONTENTS.
I. Ought Children to Ride?
II. "For Mothers & Children."
III. First Hints to a Learner.
IV. Selecting a Mount.
V., VI. The Lady's Dress.
VII. Bitting. VIII. Saddling.
IX. How to Sit, Canter, &c.
X. Reins, Voice, and Whip.
XI. Riding on the Road.
XII. Paces, Vices, and Faults.
XIII. A Lesson in Leaping.
XIV. Managing Refusers.
XV. Falling.
XVI. Hunting Outfit Considered.
XVII. Economy in Riding Dress.
XVIII. Hacks and Hunters.
XIX. In the Hunting Field.
XX. Shoeing. XXI. Feeding.
XXII. Stabling. XXIII. Doctoring.
XXIV. Breeding. XXV. "Tips."

"When there may arise differences of opinion as to some of the suggestions contained in this volume, the reader, especially if a woman, may feel assured she will not go far astray in accepting what is said by one of her own sex, who has the distinction of three times beating the Empress of Austria in the hunting field, from whom she 'took the brush.' 'Riding for Ladies' is certain to become a classic."
—*New York Sportsman.*

W. THACKER & CO., LONDON.

Ready in October, 1891.

COW KEEPING IN INDIA.
A simple and practical book on

Their care and treatment, their various breeds,

AND

THE MEANS OF RENDERING THEM PROFITABLE.

BY ISA TWEED.

CROWN 8vo.

With Thirty-Nine Illustrations, including the various Breeds of Cattle, drawn from Photographs by

R. A. STERNDALE.

THACKER, SPINK & CO., CALCUTTA.

SECOND EDITION.

In One Volume, 8vo. WITH ILLUSTRATIONS. *Rs.* 16. (25*s.*)

A Text Book of Medical Jurisprudence for India.

BY I. B. LYON, C.I.E., F.C.S., F.I.C.,

Brigade-Surgeon, Bombay Medical Service; Chemical Analyst to Government; Professor of Chemistry and Medical Jurisprudence, Grant Medical College, Bombay; Fellow of the University of Bombay.

Revised as to the legal matter by

J. D. INVERARITY,

Of the Inner Temple, Barrister-at-Law and Advocate of the High Court, Bombay.

—:o:—

CAPSICUM *(enlarged).*

"An admirable exposition of the science generally, but its special value lies in the fact that it has been written for the purpose of guidance for medical men in India. The subject matter has been arranged with great care, the classifications of poisons being especially worthy of notice."—*Lancet.*

"Will be absolutely indispensable to every member of the two professions in India, while the student will find in it everything he needs. We may congratulate Dr. Lyon on his admirable system of arrangement and the lucidity and simplicity of his style. His book is to the layman eminently readable, and probably no better book of reference has ever been prepared for professional men in India."—*Times of India.*

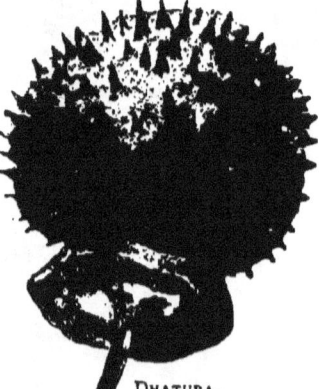

DHATURA.

"The special feature of Dr. Lyon's book is that Indian Law and Indian Practice are in each case contrasted with the Law and Practice in England, and the most conscientious care is expended in making the book absolutely exhaustive as a manual for Indian purposes. The work is a monument of industry and research.—*Home News.*"

COCCULUS INDICUS. *Enlarged.*

W. THACKER & CO., LONDON.

The Second Edition, Revised, and with additional Illustrations by the Author.
Post 8vo. *Rs.* 6. (8*s.* 6*d.*)

SEONEE:
OR,
CAMP LIFE ON THE SATPURA RANGE.

A Tale of Indian Adventure.

By R. A. STERNDALE,
AUTHOR OF "MAMMALIA OF INDIA," "DENIZENS OF THE JUNGLES."

Illustrated by the Author.

With a Map and an Appendix containing a brief Topographical and Historical account of the District of Seonee in the Central Provinces of India.

THACKER, SPINK & CO., CALCUTTA.

Oblong Imperial 4to.   *Rs.* 10. (16s.)

DENIZENS OF THE JUNGLES:

A Series of Sketches of Wild Animals,

ILLUSTRATING THEIR FORMS AND NATURAL ATTITUDES.

WITH LETTERPRESS DESCRIPTION OF EACH PLATE.

BY R. A. STERNDALE, F.R.G.S., F.Z.S.,

AUTHOR OF "NATURAL HISTORY OF THE MAMMALIA OF INDIA," "SEONEE," ETC.

I.—Denizens of the Jungles. Aborigines — Deer — Monkeys.
II.—"On the Watch." Tiger.
III.—"Not so fast Asleep as he Looks." Panther — Monkeys.
IV.—"Waiting for Father." Black Bears of the Plains
V.—"Rival Monarchs." Tiger and Elephant.
VI.—"Hors de Combat." Indian Wild Boar and Tiger.
VII.—"A Race for Life." Blue Bull and Wild Dogs.
VIII.—"Meaning Mischief." The Gaur—Indian Bison.
IX.—"More than His Match." Buffalo and Rhinoceros.
X.—"A Critical Moment." Spotted Deer and Leopard.
XI.—"Hard hit." The Sambur.
XII.—"Mountain Monarchs." Marco Polo's Sheep.

"The plates are admirably executed by photo-lithography from the author's originals, every line and touch being faithfully preserved. It is a volume which will be eagerly studied on many a table. Mr. Sterndale has many an amusing and exciting anecdote to add to the general interest of the work."—*Broad Arrow.*

"The Volume is well got up and the drawings are spirited and natural."—*Illustrated London News.*

W. THACKER & CO., LONDON.

In Imperial 16mo. Uniform with "Riding," "Riding for Ladies," "Hindu Mythology." *Rs.* 10. (12*s.* 6*d.*)

A NATURAL HISTORY
OF THE
MAMMALIA OF INDIA,
BURMAH AND CEYLON.
BY R. A. STERNDALE, F.R.G.S., F.Z.S., ETC.,
AUTHOR OF "SEONEE," "THE DENIZENS OF THE JUNGLE," "THE AFGHAN KNIFE," ETC.

WITH 170 *ILLUSTRATIONS BY THE AUTHOR AND OTHERS.*

The geographical limits of the present work have been extended to all territories likely to be reached by the sportsman from India. It is copiously illustrated, not only by the author himself, but by careful selections made by him from the works of well-known artists.

"It is the very model of what a popular natural history should be."—*Knowledge.*
"An amusing work with good illustrations."—*Nature.*
"Full of accurate observation, brightly told."—*Saturday Review.*
"The results of a close and sympathetic observation."—*Athenæum.*
"It has the brevity which is the soul of wit, and a delicacy of allusion which charms the literary critic."—*Academy.*
"The notices of each animal are, as a rule, short, though on some of the larger mammals—the lion, tiger, pard, boar, &c.—ample and interesting details are given, including occasional anecdotes of adventure. The book will, no doubt, be specially useful to the sportsman, and, indeed, has been extended so as to include all territories likely to be reached by the sportsman from India. Those who desire to obtain some general information, popularly conveyed, on the subject with which the book deals, will, we believe, find it useful."—*The Times.*
"Has contrived to hit a happy mean between the stiff scientific treatise and the bosh of what may be called anecdotal zoology."—*The Daily News.*

THACKER, SPINK & CO., CALCUTTA.

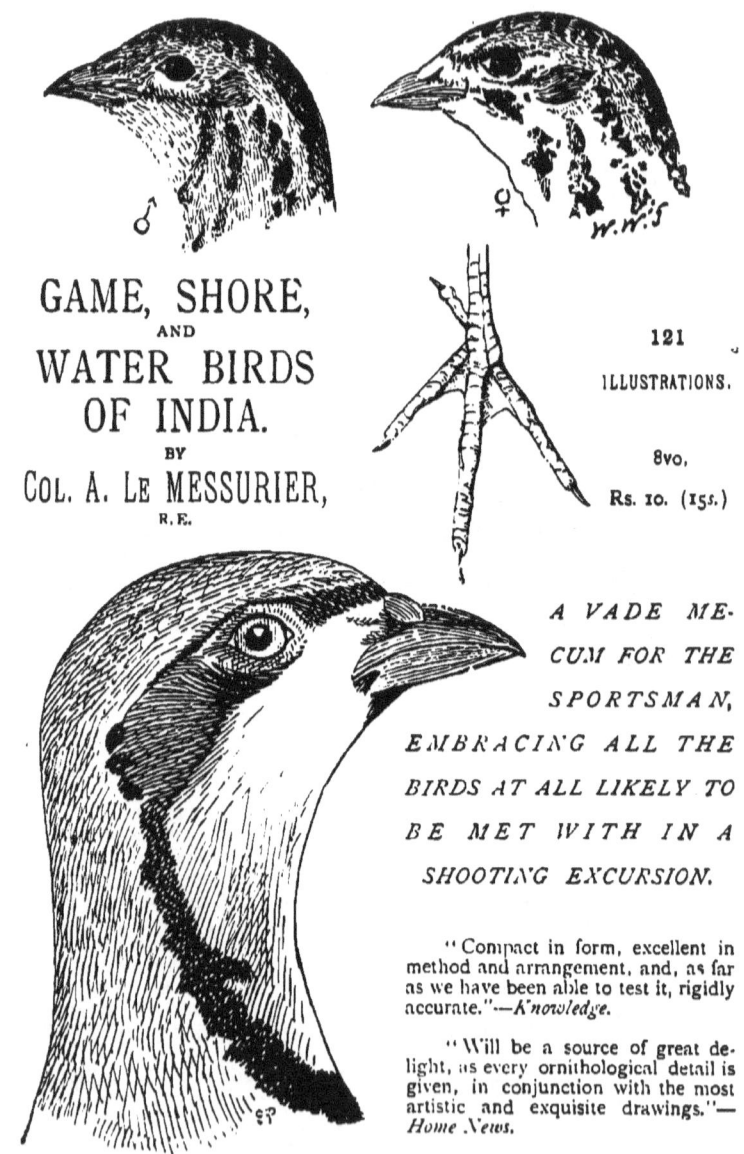

GAME, SHORE,
AND
WATER BIRDS OF INDIA.
BY
Col. A. Le MESSURIER,
R.E.

121 ILLUSTRATIONS.

8vo,

Rs. 10. (15s.)

A VADE ME-CUM FOR THE SPORTSMAN, EMBRACING ALL THE BIRDS AT ALL LIKELY TO BE MET WITH IN A SHOOTING EXCURSION.

"Compact in form, excellent in method and arrangement, and, as far as we have been able to test it, rigidly accurate."—*Knowledge.*

"Will be a source of great delight, as every ornithological detail is given, in conjunction with the most artistic and exquisite drawings."—*Home News.*

W. THACKER & CO., LONDON

"Splendidly Illustrated Record of Sport."—*Graphic.*

In Demy 4to. Thirty Plates and Map. *Rs.* 25. (£2 2s.)

LARGE GAME SHOOTING

IN THIBET AND THE NORTH-WEST.

By COLONEL ALEXANDER A. KINLOCH.

Reduced from the Photo-Lithographed Original.

"Colonel Kinloch, who has killed most kinds of Indian game, small and great, relates incidents of his varied sporting experiences in chapters, which are each descriptive of a different animal. The photo-gravures of the heads of many of the animals, from the grand gaur, popularly miscalled the bison, downwards, are extremely clever and spirited."—*Times.*

LAYS OF IND. By Aliph Cheem.

COMIC, SATIRICAL, AND DESCRIPTIVE

Poems Illustrative of Anglo-Indian Life.

ILLUSTRATED BY THE AUTHOR, LIONEL INGLIS, R. A. STERNDALE, AND OTHERS.

Eighth Edition. Cloth, gilt. Rs. 7-8. (10s. 6d.)

"This is a remarkably bright little book. 'Aliph Cheem, supposed to be the *nom de plume* of an officer in the 18th Hussars, is, after his fashion, an Indian Bon Gaultier. In a few of the poems the jokes, turning on local names and customs, are somewhat esoteric; but, taken throughout, the verses are characterized by high animal spirits, great cleverness, and most excellent fooling."—*The World.*

"Aliph Cheem presents us in this volume with some highly amusing ballads and songs, which have already in a former edition warmed the hearts and cheered the lonely hours of many an Anglo-Indian, the pictures being chiefly those of Indian life. There is no mistaking the humour, and at times, indeed, the fun is both 'fast and furious.' Many portions remind us of the 'Bab Ballads.' One can readily imagine the merriment created round the camp fire by the recitation of 'The Two Thumpers,' which is irresistibly droll. . . . The edition before us is enlarged, and contains illustrations by the author, in addition to which it is beautifully printed and handsomely got up, all which recommendations are sure to make the name of Aliph Cheem more popular in India than ever."—*Liverpool Mercury.*

W. THACKER & CO., LONDON.

Reviews of "Lays of Ind."

"The 'Lays' are not only Anglo-Indian in origin, but out-and-out Anglo-Indian in subject and colour. To one who knows something of life at an Indian 'station' they will be especially amusing. Their exuberant fun at the same time may well attract the attention of the ill-defined individual known as 'the general reader.'"—*Scotsman.*

"To many Anglo-Indians the lively verses of 'Aliph Cheem' must be very well known, while to those who have not yet become acquainted with them we can only say read them on the first opportunity. To those not familiar with Indian life they may be specially commended for the picture which they give of many of its lighter incidents and conditions, and of several of its ordinary personages. . . . We have read the volume with real pleasure, and we have only to add that it is nicely printed and elegantly finished, and that it has several charming woodcuts, of which some are by the author, whom Indian gossip, by the way, has identified with Captain Yeldham, of the 18th Hussars."—*Bath Chronicle.*

"Satire of the most amusing and inoffensive kind, humour the most genuine, and pathos the most touching pervade these 'Lays of Ind.' . . . From Indian friends we have heard of the popularity these 'Lays' have obtained in the land where they were written and we predict for them a popularity equally great at home."—*Monthly Homœopathic Review.*

"The author, although assuming a *nom de plume*, is recognised as a distinguished cavalry officer, possessed of a vivid imagination and a sense of humour amounting sometimes to rollicking and contagious fun. Many of his 'Lays' suggest recollections of some of the best pieces in the 'Ingoldsby Legends,' or in the 'Biglow Papers' of Russell Lowell, while revealing a character of their own."—*Capital and Labour.*

THACKER, SPINK & CO., CALCUTTA.

New Edition, Demy 8vo, with all Original Illustrations. Rs. 7-8.

THE HIGHLANDS OF CENTRAL INDIA.

Wood Cuts and

NOTES ON THEIR FORESTS AND WILD TRIBES, NATURAL HISTORY AND SPORT.

Coloured Plates.

BY CAPT. J. FORSYTH, BENGAL STAFF CORPS.
ILLUSTRATIONS BY R. A. STERNDALE, F.Z.S., F.R.G.S.

W. THACKER & CO., LONDON.

Crown 8vo. Buckram. Rs. 9 (12s. 6d.)
Fourth Edition, revised to the latest Science of the day, with many new Illustrations.

VETERINARY NOTES
FOR HORSE-OWNERS.
A Handbook of Veterinary Medicine and Surgery, written in Popular Language.
BY CAPT. M. H. HAYES, F.R.C.V.S.

The chief new matter in this edition is—articles on Contracted Heels, Donkey's Foot Disease, Forging or Clicking, Rheumatic Joint Disease, Abscess, Dislocation of the Shoulder Joint, Inflammation of the Mouth and Tongue, Flatulent Distention of the Stomach, Twist of the Intestines, Relapsing Fever, Cape Horse Sickness, Horse Syphilis, Rabies, Megrims, Staggers, Epilepsy, Sunstroke, Poisoning, Castration by the Écraseur, and Mechanism of the Foot (in Chapter on Shoeing). The remarks on Treatment of Sprain (with special reference to cotton wool bandaging), Grease and Cracked Heels, Wounds and their Results, Broken Wind, Roaring, Rheumatism and Neurotomy have been re-written. The whole work has been revised with the greatest care.

—:o:—

"Of the many popular veterinary books which have come under our notice, this is certainly one of the most scientific and reliable. The description of symptoms and the directions for the application of remedies are given in perfectly plain terms, which the tyro will find no difficulty in comprehending; and, for the purpose of further smoothing his path, a chapter is given on veterinary medicines, their actions, uses, and doses. This information will be most acceptable to the majority of horse-owners, and may be invaluable in an emergency when no advice better than that of the village cow doctor can be obtained."—*The Field.*
"We do not think that horse-owners in general are likely to find a more reliable or useful book for guidance in an emergency."—*The Field.*
"The work is written in a clear and practical way."—*Saturday Review.*

Third Edition. Revised and Enlarged. Imperial 16mo. Rs. 7-8 (10s. 6d).

RIDING:
ON THE FLAT AND ACROSS COUNTRY.

A GUIDE TO PRACTICAL HORSEMANSHIP. By CAPT. M. H. HAYES.

Eighty Illustrations by Oswald Brown, Sturgess and S. Berkeley.

W. THACKER & CO., LONDON.

(*Reduced Size.*)

Third Edition.

—:o:—

REVISED
AND ENLARGED

—:o:—

Imperial 16mo.

Rs. 7-8 (10*s.* 6*d.*).

RIDING:
ON THE FLAT AND ACROSS COUNTRY.
A Guide to Practical Horsemanship.
BY CAPT. M. H. HAYES, F.R.C.V.S.

*Eighty
Illustra-
tions*

BY

*Oswald
Brown,
Sturgess*
AND
*Stanley
Berkeley.*

(*Reduced Size.*)

THACKER, SPINK & CO., CALCUTTA.

Uniform with Captain Hayes' "Riding."

THE HORSEWOMAN

A PRACTICAL GUIDE TO SIDE-SADDLE RIDING.

By Mrs. HAYES.   Edited by Captain M. H. HAYES.
With Numerous Collotype Illustrations and Drawings from
Photographs by OSWALD BROWN.
Imperial 16mo.   Rs. 7-8.   (10s. 6d.)

THE HORSEWOMAN. By Mrs. and Capt. Hayes.

A PRACTICAL GUIDE TO SIDE-SADDLE RIDING.

Uniform with "Riding: on the Flat and Across Country." Rs. 7-8. (10s. 6d.)

ILLUSTRATED HORSE-BREAKING.

BY

CAPT. M. H. HAYES.

Uniform with "Riding," &c. *Rs.* 16. (21*s.*)

ILLUSTRATED HORSE-BREAKING

BY

Capt. M. H. HAYES.

1. Theory of Breaking.
2. Principles of Mounting.
3. Horse Control.
4. Rendering Docile.
5. Giving Good Mouths.
6. Teaching to Jump.
7. Mount for First Time.
8. Breaking for Ladies' Riding.
9. Breaking to Harness.
10. Faults of Mouth.
11. Nervousness and Impatience.
12. Jibbing.
13. Jumping Faults.
14 Faults in Harness.
15. Aggressiveness.
16. Riding and Driving Newly-broken Horse.
17. Stable Vices.

"Far and away the best reasoned-out book on breaking under a new system we have seen."—*Field.*

"Clearly explained in simp'e, practical language, made all the more clear by a set of capital drawings."—*Scotsman.*

WITH FIFTY-ONE ILLUSTRATIONS BY J. H. OSWALD BROWN.

THACKER, SPINK & CO., CALCUTTA.

Crown 8vo. Uniform with "Veterinary Notes." *Rs.* 6. (8*s*. 6*d*.)

SOUNDNESS AND AGE OF HORSES.

WITH ONE HUNDRED AND SEVENTY ILLUSTRATIONS.

A Complete Guide to all those features which require attention when purchasing Horses, distinguishing mere defects from the symptoms of unsoundness; with explicit instructions how to conduct an examination of the various parts.

BY CAPTAIN M. HORACE HAYES, F.R.C.V.S.,

AUTHOR OF "RIDING," "VETERINARY NOTES," "TRAINING AND HORSE MANAGEMENT," ETC.

W. THACKER & CO., LONDON.

In Imperial 16mo. Illustrated. *Rs.* 6. (8*s.* 6*d.*)

INDIAN RACING REMINISCENCES:
BEING
ENTERTAINING NARRATIVES AND ANECDOTES OF MEN, HORSES, AND SPORT.

Illustrated with Twenty-Two Portraits and a Number of Smaller Engravings.

BY M. HORACE HAYES.

"The book is full of racy anecdote, and the author writes so k'ndly of his brother officers and the sporting planters with whom he came into contact, that one cannot help admiring the genial and happy temperament of the author."—*Bell's Life.*

"Captain Hayes shows himself a thorough master of his subject, and has so skilfully interwoven technicalities, history, and anecdote, that the last page comes all too soon."—*Field.*

Fourth Edition. Revised. Crown 8vo. *Rs.* 5. (7*s.* 6*d.*)

TRAINING & HORSE MANAGEMENT
IN INDIA.
BY CAPTAIN M. HORACE HAYES.

"No better guide could be placed in the hands of either amateur horseman or veterinary surgeon."—*The Veterinary Journal.*

"A useful guide in regard to horses anywhere. . . . Concise, practical, and portab'e."
—*Saturday Review.*

THE POINTS OF THE HORSE:
A Familiar Treatise on Equine Formation.
By CAPTAIN M. HORACE HAYES.

Illustrated by J. H. OSWALD BROWN, describing the points in which the perfection of each class of horses consists. Together with very numerous reproductions of living Typical Animals, with contrasting Illustrations from Photographs, forming an invaluable guide to owners of horses.

THACKER, SPINK & CO., CALCUTTA.

IN IMPERIAL 16mo.

MY LEPER FRIENDS.

AN ACCOUNT OF

PERSONAL WORK AMONG LEPERS,

AND

THEIR DAILY LIFE IN INDIA.

By Mrs. HAYES.

—:o:—

WITH A

CHAPTER ON LEPROSY

BY

Surgeon-Major

G. G. MACLAREN, M.D.

Illustrated by reproductions of Photographs.

W. THACKER & CO., LONDON.

Uniform with "Lays of Ind," "Riding," etc. *Rs.* 7-8. (10s. 6d.)

HINDU MYTHOLOGY:
VEDIC AND PURANIC.

BY

REV. W. J. WILKINS,

OF THE LONDON MISSIONARY SOCIETY, CALCUTTA.

Illustrated by One Hundred Engravings chiefly from Drawings by Native Artists.

REVIEWS.

"His aim has been to give a faithful account of the Hindu deities such as an intelligent native would himself give, and he has endeavoured, in order to achieve his purpose, to keep his mind free from prejudice or theological bias. To help to completeness he has included a number of drawings of the principal deities, executed by native artists. The author has attempted a work of no little ambition and has succeeded in his attempt, the volume being one of great interest and usefulness; and not the less so because he has strictly refrained from diluting his facts with comments of his own. It has numerous illustrations."—*Home News.*

"Mr. Wilkins has done his work well, with an honest desire to state facts apart from all theological prepossession, and his volume is likely to be a useful book of reference."—*Guardian.*

"In Mr. Wilkins' book we have an illustrated manual, the study of which will lay a solid foundation for more advanced knowledge, while it will furnish those who may have the desire without having the time or opportunity to go further into the subject, with a really extensive stock of accurate information."—*Indian Daily News.*

H. E. BUSTEED'S "ECHOES FROM OLD CALCUTTA."

A MOST INTERESTING SERIES OF SKETCHES OF CALCUTTA LIFE, CHIEFLY TOWARDS THE CLOSE OF THE LAST CENTURY. Post 8vo. Rs. 6. (8s. 6d.)

Door of Black Hole.   Grated Windows.

THE "BLACK HOLE" OF CALCUTTA.

W. THACKER & CO., LONDON.

In Post 8vo, uniform with "Seonee." *Rs.* 6. (8*s.* 6*d.*)

A NEW AND ILLUSTRATED EDITION

OF

ECHOES FROM OLD CALCUTTA.

BY

DR. H. E. BUSTEED, M.D., C.I.E.

"We hear that Dr. H. E. BUSTEED, whose charming little book on 'Old Calcutta' commanded a deserved popularity among Indian readers, is now engaged in his retirement at home in bringing out a new edition, which will be much amplified, and illustrated by portraits of ladies and gentlemen of the settlement who were local celebrities a century ago. Dr. BUSTEED has devoted himself to research with indefatigable industry, and fortunately his literary style is as graceful and entertaining as his knowledge is profound and accurate."—*Calcutta Englishman.*

"It is a pleasure to reiterate the warm commendation of this instructive and lively volume which its appearance called forth some few years since. It would be lamentable if a book so fraught with interest to all Englishmen should be restricted to Anglo-Indian circles. A fresh instalment of letters from Warren Hastings to his wife must be noted as extremely interesting, while the papers on Sir Philip Francis, Nuncomar, and the romantic career of Mrs. Grand, who became Princess Benevento and the wife of Talleyrand, ought to by now to be widely known."—*Saturday Review.*

"Dr. Busteed has unearthed some astonishing revelations of what European Life in India resembled a century back. Perhaps for the first time has the Black Hole drama been told in a way fully to bring home to the mind the appalling nature of the sufferings undergone by our countrymen and countrywomen."—*Daily Telegraph.*

CHAPTERS:
I.—THE BLACK HOLE.—THE CAPTURE OF CALCUTTA.
II.—THE BLACK HOLE.—THE IMPRISONMENT.
III.—PHILIP FRANCIS AND HIS TIMES—1. ARRIVAL IN CALCUTTA.
IV.—   ,,   2. NUNCOMAR.
V.—   ,,   3. DUEL BETWEEN FRANCIS AND HASTINGS.
VI.—   ,,   4. HOME AND SOCIAL LIFE.
VII.—THE FIRST INDIAN NEWSPAPER.   VIII.—MADAME GRAND.
IX.—LETTERS FROM WARREN HASTINGS TO HIS WIFE.
X —LETTERS FROM MRS. HASTINGS.   XI.—AN OLD CALCUTTA GRAVE.

THE CULTURE AND MANUFACTURE OF INDIGO:

With Description of a Planter's Life and Resources. By W. M. REID. *With Nineteen Illustrations by the Author.* Rs. 5. (7s. 6d.)

"A concise and readable manual, not only of everything relating to the industry, but of the whole round of business and recreation that makes up the Planter's life. . . . The writer is at once accurate and graphic, and on the strength merely of reading these bright pages one almost feels competent to take full charge of a 'concern.'"—*Englishman.*

W. THACKER & CO., LONDON.

Crown 8vo. *Rs.* 5-8. (7s. 6d.)

A TEA PLANTER'S LIFE IN ASSAM.
By GEORGE M. BARKER.
WITH SEVENTY-FIVE ILLUSTRATIONS BY THE AUTHOR.

This book aims at conveying to all interested in India and the tea industry an entertaining and useful account of the topographical features of Assam; the strange surroundings—human and animal—of the European resident; the trying climate; the daily life of the planter; and general details of the formation and working of tea gardens.

"Mr. Barker has supplied us with a very good and readable description, accompanied by numerous illustrations drawn by himself. What may be called the business parts of the book are of most value."—*Contemporary Review.*

"Cheery, well-written little book."—*Graphic.*

"A very interesting and amusing book, artistically illustrated from sketches drawn by the author."—*Mark Lane Express.*

List of the Tea Gardens of India and Ceylon. Their Acreage, Managers, Assistants, Calcutta Agents, Coolie Depôts, Proprietors, Companies, Directors, Capital, London Agents and Factory Marks, by which any chest may be identified. Also embraces Coffee, Indigo, Silk, Sugar, Cinchona, Lac, Cardamom and other Concerns. 8vo. Sewed. 6r. 6d.

"The strong point of the book is the reproduction of the factory marks, which are presented side by side with the letterpress. To buyers of tea and other Indian products on this side, the work needs no recommendation."—*British Trade Journal.*

THACKER, SPINK & CO., CALCUTTA.

PRICE 6s. 6d.   8vo, SEWED.

—:o:—

A COMPLETE LIST

OF THE

TEA GARDENS

OF

INDIA AND CEYLON.

CONTAINING THEIR

FACTORY

ACREAGE		PROPRIETORS
MANAGERS	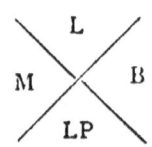	COMPANIES,
ASSISTANTS		DIRECTORS
CALCUTTA AGENTS		CAPITAL
COOLIE DEPOTS		LONDON AGENTS

MARKS

By which any Chest may be identified.

ALSO EMBRACES

Coffee, Indigo, Silk, Sugar, Cinchona, Lac, Cardamom,

AND OTHER CONCERNS.

W. THACKER & CO., LONDON.

In Demy folio,
Thirty-nine Plates
beautifully executed by the
University Press, Edinburgh.

Rs. 16. (25*s.*)

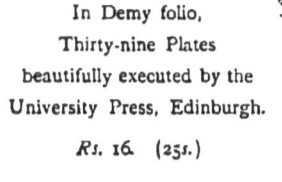

ILLUSTRATIONS
OF THE
GRASSES
OF THE
SOUTHERN PUNJAB.
BEING

Photo-Lithographs of Some of the Principal Grasses Found at Hissar.

WITH

SHORT DESCRIPTIVE LETTERPRESS,

BY WILLIAM COLDSTREAM, B.A., B.C.S.,
Fellow of the Punjab University and Member of the Royal Botanical Society of Edinburgh.

Reduced from Original.

THACKER, SPINK & CO., CALCUTTA.

300 *Illustrations. Imperial 16mo. Rs.* 10. (12s. 6d.)

Uniform with "Lays of Ind," "Hindu Mythology," "Riding," "Natural History of the Mammalia of India," etc.

A POPULAR HANDBOOK
OF
INDIAN FERNS.

By COLONEL R. H. BEDDOME,

AUTHOR OF THE "FERNS OF BRITISH INDIA," "THE FERNS OF SOUTHERN INDIA."

"It is the first special book of portable size and moderate price which has been devoted to Indian Ferns, and is in every way deserving of the extensive circulation it is sure to obtain."—*Nature.*

"I have just seen a new work on Indian Ferns which will prove vastly interesting, not only to the Indian people, but to the botanists of this country."—*Indian Daily News.*

"The 'Ferns of India.' This is a good book, being of a useful and trustworthy character. The species are familiarly described, and most of them illustrated by small figures."—*Gardeners' Chronicle.*

"Those interested in botany will do well to procure a new work on the 'Ferns of British India.' The work will prove a first-class text book."—*Free Press.*

THREE HUNDRED ILLUSTRATIONS BY THE AUTHOR.

Complete in One Volume, Rs. 5. (7s. 6d.); Interleaved, Rs. 5-8. (8s. 6d.)

A TEXT BOOK
OF
INDIAN BOTANY:
MORPHOLOGICAL,
PHYSIOLOGICAL,
and SYSTEMATIC.

BY W. H. GREGG,
LECTURER ON BOTANY, HUGHLI COLLEGE.

WITH 240 ILLUSTRATIONS.

Crown 8vo. Rs. 5. (7s. 6d.)

MANUAL OF
AGRICULTURE FOR INDIA.
BY LIEUT. F. POGSON.

---

1. Origin and Character of Soils.—2. Ploughing and Preparing for Seed.—3. Manures and Composts.—4. Wheat Cultivation.—5. Barley.—6. Oats. —7. Rye.—8. Rice.—9. Maize.—10. Sugar-producing Sorghums.—11. Common Sorghums.—12. Sugarcane.—13. Oil Seed.—14. Field Pea Crops.—15. Dall or Pulse.—16. Root Crops.—17. Cold Spice.—18. Fodder.—19. Water-Nut.—20. Ground-Nut.—21. Rush-Nut or Chufas.—22. Cotton.—23. Tobacco.—24. Mensuration.—Appendix.

"A work of extreme practical value."—*Home News.*

"Mr. Pogson's advice may be profitably followed by both native and European agriculturists, for it is eminently practical and devoid of empiricism. His little volume embodies the teaching of a large and varied experience, and deserves to be warmly supported."—*Madras Mail.*

THACKER, SPINK & CO., CALCUTTA.

Fourth Edition, Imperial 16mo. *Rs.* 10. (15*s.*)

A MANUAL OF GARDENING
FOR
BENGAL AND UPPER INDIA.
By THOMAS A. C. FIRMINGER, M.A.

THOROUGHLY REVISED AND BROUGHT DOWN TO THE PRESENT TIME BY

J. H. JACKSON,
Editor of " The Indian Agriculturist."

PART I.

OPERATIONS OF GARDENING.

Chap. I.—Climate—Soils—Manures.
Chap. II.—Laying-out a Garden—Lawns—Hedges—Hoeing and Digging—Drainage — Conservatories — Betel Houses—Decorations—Implements—Shades—Labels—Vermin—Weeds.
Chap. III.—Seeds—Seed Sowing—Pot Culture—Planting—Cuttings—Layers—Gootee—Grafting and Inarching—Budding—Pruning and Root Pruning—Conveyance.
Chap. IV.—Calendar of Operations.

PART II.

GARDEN PLANTS.

1. Culinary Vegetables.
2. Dessert Fruits.
3. Edible Nuts.
4. Ornamental Annuals.
5. Ornamental Trees, Shrubs, and Herbaceous Perennials.

Crown 8vo, cloth. *Rs.* 2-8.

THE AMATEUR GARDENER IN THE HILLS.

HINTS FROM VARIOUS AUTHORITIES ON GARDEN MANAGEMENT, AND ADAPTED TO THE HILLS;

WITH HINTS ON FOWLS, PIGEONS, AND RABBIT KEEPING;

And various Recipes connected with the above subjects which are not commonly found in Recipe Books.

W. THACKER & CO., LONDON.

Thacker's Guide Books.

Agra and its Neighbourhood: A Handbook for Visitors. By H. G. KEENE, C.S. Fifth Edition, Revised. Maps, Plans, &c. Fcap. 8vo, cloth. Rs. 2-8.

Allahabad, Cawnpore and Lucknow. By H. G. KEENE, C.S. Second Edition, Re-written and Enlarged. Fcap. 8vo.

Burma and its People, Manners, Customs and Religion. By Capt. C. J. V. S. FORBES. 8vo. Rs. 4 (7s. 6d.).

Burmah Myam-Ma: the Home of the Burman. By TSAYA (Rev. H. POWELL). Crown 8vo. Rs. 2 (3s. 6d.).

Calcutta, Thacker's Guide to. With Chapters on its Bypaths, &c., and a Chapter on the Government of India. Fcap. 8vo, With Maps. Rs. 3.

Calcutta to Liverpool by China, Japan and America, in 1877. By Lieut.-General Sir HENRY NORMAN. Second Edition. Fcap. 8vo, cloth. Rs. 2-8 (3s. 6d.).
The only book published on this interesting route between India and England.

Darjeeling and its Neighbourhood. By S. MITCHELL, M.A. With two Maps. Rs. 2.

Delhi and its Neighbourhood, A Handbook for Visitors to. By H. G. KEENE, C.S. Third Edition. Maps. Fcap. 8vo, cloth. Rs. 2-8.

India, Thacker's Map, in case, 8s. 6d.

India, Map of the Civil Divisions of; including Governments, Divisions and Districts, Political Agencies and Native States; also the Cities and Towns. Re. 1.

Kashmir Handbook (Ince's). Revised and Re-written. By Surg.-Major JOSHUA DUKE. With 4 Maps. Fcap. 8vo, cloth. Rs. 6.

Kashgaria (Eastern or Chinese Turkestan), Historical, Geographical, Military and Industrial. By Col. KUROPATKIN, Russian Army. Translated by Major GOWAN, H. M.'s Indian Army. 8vo. Rs. 6-8 (10s. 6d.).

Kumaun Lakes, Angling in the. With a Map of the Kumaun Lake Country. By Depy. Surg.-Genl. W. WALKER. Crown 8vo, cloth. Rs. 4.
"Written with all the tenderness and attention to detail which characterise the followers of the gentle art."—*Hayes' Sporting News.*

Masuri, Landaur, Dehra Dun, and the Hills North of Dehra; including Routes to the Snows and other places of note; with chapter on Garhwal (Tehri), Hardwar, Rurki, and Chakrata. By JOHN NORTHAM. Rs. 2-8.

Simla, The Hills beyond. Three Months' Tour from Simla ("In the Footsteps of the Few") through Bussahir, Kunowar, and Spiti, to Lahoul. By Mrs. J. C. MURRAY-AYNSLEY. Crown 8vo, cloth. Rs. 3.

Gold, Copper and Lead in Chota Nagpore. Compiled by Dr. W. KING, Director Geological Survey of India, and T. A. POPE, Dep. Supt. Survey of India. With Map of Geological Formation and the Areas taken up by the various Prospecting and Mining Companies. Crown 8vo, cloth. Rs. 5 (10s.).

Russian Conversation - Grammar (on the System of Otto). With Exercises, Colloquial Phrases, and an English - Russian Vocabulary. By A. KINLOCH, late Interpreter to H. B. M. Consulate, St. Petersburg. Rs. 6-8 (9s.).
Constructed on the excellent system of Otto, with Illustrations accompanying every rule in the form of usual phrases and idioms; thus leading the Student by easy and rapid gradations to a colloquial knowledge of the Language.

THACKER, SPINK & CO., CALCUTTA.

The Reconnoitrer's Guide and Field Book, adapted for India. By Major M. J. KING-HARMAN, B.S.C. Second Edition, Revised and Enlarged. In roan. *Rs.* 4.
Can be used as an ordinary Pocket Note Book, or as a Field Message Book; the pages are ruled as a Field Book, and in sections, for written description or sketch. " To officers serving in India this guide will be invaluable."—*Broad Arrow.*

Atlas of Clinical Medicine. By BYRON BRAMWELL, M.D, F.R.C.P., Edin.; Assistant Physician to the Edinburgh Royal Infirmary. Four parts per annum, issued to Yearly Subscribers only, and the entire work is expected to extend to 3 vols, forming an Illustrated Treatise on Clinical and Systematic Medicine. Each yearly vol. will be complete in itself, and may be had separately.

Tales from Indian History: being the Annals of India retold in Narratives. By J. TALBOYS WHEELER. Sixth Edition. Crown 8vo, cloth gilt. *Rs.* 2-8 (3*s.* 6*d.*).

Hindustani as it ought to be Spoken. A Manual with Explanations, Vocabularies and Exercises. By J. TWEEDIE, C.S. *Rs.* 2-8 (5*s.*).

A Memoir of the late Justice Onoocool Chunder Mookerjee. By M. MOOKERJEE. Third Edition. 12mo. *Re.* 1 (2*s.* 6*d.*).
A most interesting and amusing illustration of Indian English.
"The reader is earnestly advised to procure the life of this gentleman, written by his nephew, and read it."—*The Tribes on my Frontier.*

The Indian Cookery Book. A Practical Handbook to the Kitchen in India: adapted to the Three Presidencies. By a Thirty-five Years' Resident. *Rs.* 3 (4*s.* 6*d.*).

Indian Notes about Dogs: their Diseases and Treatment. By Major C——. Third Edition, Revised. Fcap. 8vo, cloth. *Rs.* 1-8.

Indian Horse Notes: an Epitome of useful Information. By Major C——, Author of " Indian Notes about Dogs." Second Edition, Enlarged. Fcap. 8vo, cloth. *Rs.* 2.

Horse-Breeding and Rearing in India: with Notes on Training for the Flat and Across Country; and on Purchase, Breaking-in, and General Management. By Major J. HUMFREY. Crown 8vo. *Rs.* 3-8 (6*s.*).

Indian Idyls. The Maharajah's Guest and other Tales. By an Idle Exile. Mrs. E. E. CUTHELL. *Rs.* 2-8 (5*s.*).

The Inspector; a Comedy. By GOGOL. Translated from the Russian. By HART-DAVIES, Bombay Civil Service. *Rs.* 2 (4*s.*).

Hygiene of Water and Water Supplies. By PATRICK HEHIR, M.D., F.R.C.S. Edin.; Lecturer on Hygiene, Hydembad. Surgeon, Bengal Army. 8vo, limp cloth. *Rs.* 2.

Plain Tales from the Hills: A Collection of Stories by RUDYARD KIPLING. Third Edition. Crown 8vo. *Rs.* 4.
"They sparkle with fun; they are full of life, merriment and humour."—*Allen's Indian Mail.*

Departmental Ditties and other Verses. By RUDYARD KIPLING. Being Humorous Poems of Indian Officialdom. Sixth Edition. In square 32mo. *Rs.* 2-8 (5*s.*).
" . . . . His book gives hope of a new literary star of no mean magnitude rising in the east."—*Sir W. W. Hunter in " The Academy."*

The Management and Medical Treatment of Children in India. By EDWARD A. BIRCH, M.D., Surg.-Major, Bengal Establishment. Second Edition Revised (Being the Eighth Edition of "Goodeve's Hints"). Crown 8vo. *Rs.* 7. (10*s.* 6*d.*)

Our Administration of India. Being a Complete Account of the Revenue and Collectorate Administration in all Departments, with special reference to the Work and Duties of a District Officer in Bengal. By H. A. D. PHILLIPS. *Rs.* 4-4 (6*s.*).

W. THACKER & CO., LONDON.

PUBLISHED IN CALCUTTA ANNUALLY.

Super Royal 8vo. Leather backs, Rs. 20. (36s.)

THACKER'S INDIAN DIRECTORY,

EMBRACING THE WHOLE EMPIRE GOVERNED BY THE VICEROY OF INDIA, AND ALSO THE NATIVE STATES.

With Complete and Detailed Information of the Cities of Calcutta, Bombay and Madras.

WITH ALMANAC, ARMY LIST, AND GENERAL INFORMATION.

From the London "TIMES."

"'The work now' includes in the Mofussil Directory an account of every district and principal town in British and Foreign India, and every native State,' thus forming a complete guide to the whole of our possessions in the East. The value of such a work, if it is accurate and trustworthy, is obvious, and almost goes without saying ; and, after putting its pages to the test of a careful scrutiny where our personal experience enables us to do so, we are able to pronounce it apparently deserving of all commendation. . . . The alphabetical list of residents throughout India in the three great provinces, with their addresses, must be of great service to those who have business with our Eastern Empire."

THE INDIAN
MEDICAL GAZETTE,

A Record of Medicine, Surgery, and Public Health, and of General Medical Intelligence, Indian and European.

Edited by K. McLEOD, M.D.

Published Monthly. Subscriptions Rs. 18 per Annum, including Postage.

The *Indian Medical Gazette* has earned for itself a world-wide reputation by its solid contributions to Tropical Medicine and Surgery. It is the sole representative medium for recording the work and experience of the Medical Profession in India ; and its arrangements with all the leading Medical Journals in Great Britain and America enable it not only to diffuse this information broadcast throughout the world, but also to cull for its Indian readers, from an unusual variety of sources, all information which has any practical bearing on medical works in India.

It is indispensable to every Member of the Medical Profession in India who wishes to keep himself abreast of medical progress.

INDEX.

Title	Rs.		Page
"Amateur Gardener in the Hills."	2-8	...	36
Barker. "Tea Planter in Assam."	5-8	7/6	31
Beddome. "Ferns of India."	10	12/6	34
Bramwell. "Atlas Clinical Medicine."	...	...	38
Birch. "Children in India."	7	10 6	38
Busteed. "Echoes from Old Calcutta"	6	8/6	28
Coldstream. "Grasses of the Punjab."	16	25/-	33
Eha. "Behind the Bungalow."	4-8	6/-	2
,, "Tribes on my Frontier."	6	8 6	4
Firminger. "Gardening for India." By Jackson.	10	15/-	36
Forsyth. "Highlands of Central India."	7-8	...	16
Guide Books.	...	...	37
Gogol. "The Inspector." Translated. By Hart-Davies.	2	4/-	38
Gregg. "Indian Botany."	5	7 6	35
Hayes. "Veterinary Notes."	9	12 6	17
,, "Riding."	7-8	10 6	18
,, "Horsewoman."	7-8	10 6	20
,, "Illustrated Horse-Breaking."	16	21/-	22
,, "Soundness and Age."	6	8-6	24
,, "Indian Racing."	6	8/6	25
,, "Training and Horse Management."	5	7/6	25
,, "Points of the Horse."	...	...	25
,, "My Leper Friends."	...	...	26
Humfrey. "Horse-Breeding."	2-8	...	38
Hehir. "Hygiene of Water."	2	...	38
"Indian Idyls."	2-8	5/-	38
"Indian Cookery."	3	4 6	38
"Indian Notes—Dogs."	1-8	...	38
"Indian ,, Horses."	2	...	38
"Indian Medical Gazette." Subscription.	18	...	39
King and Pope. "Gold, Copper, Lead," &c.	5	10/-	37
Kinloch. "Large Game."	25	42/	13
,, "Russian Grammar."	6-8	9/-	37
King-Harman. "Reconnoitring."	4	...	38
Kipling. "Plain Tales."	4	...	38
,, "Departmental Ditties."	2-8	5/-	38
Le Messurier. "Game Birds."	10	15/-	12
Lyon. "Medical Jurisprudence."	16	25/-	8
"Lays of Ind." By Aliph Cheem.	7-8	10 6	14
O'Donoghue. "Riding for Ladies."	7-8	10 6	6
"Onoocool Mookerjee, Life of."	1	2 6	38
Phillips. "Our Administration of India."	4-4	6/-	38
Pogson. "Agriculture for India."	5	7 6	35
Reid. "Indigo Planter."	5	7/6	30
Sterndale. "Denizens of the Jungle."	10	16/-	10
,, "Mammalia of India."	10	12/6	11
,, "Seonee."	6	8 6	9
"Tea Gardens of India and Ceylon."	...	6 6	32
Thacker's Guide Books, various.	...	...	37
,, "Indian Directory."	...	36/-	39
,, "Map of India."	...	...	37
Tweedie. "How to Speak Hindustani."	2-8	5/-	38
Tweed. "Cow Keeping in India."	...	...	7
Wilkins. "Hindu Mythology."	7-8	10 6	27
Wheeler. "Tales Indian History."	2-8	3 6	38

www.ingramcontent.com/pod-product-compliance
Lightning Source LLC
Chambersburg PA
CBHW032149160426
43197CB00008B/836